NAVIGATION

Navigation

Selected Poems
1985–2010

DENNIS PHILLIPS

with an Afterword by George Albon

OTIS BOOKS | SEISMICITY EDITIONS

The Graduate Writing program
Otis College of Art and Design
LOS ANGELES ● 2011

Book design and typesetting: Rebecca Chamlee

ISBN: 0-9845289-4-6
ISBN 13: 978-0-9845289-4-3

OTIS BOOKS | SEISMICITY EDITIONS
The Graduate Writing program
Otis College of Art and Design
9045 Lincoln Boulevard
Los Angeles, CA 90045

http://gw.otis.edu
seismicity@otis.edu
https://blogs.otis.edu/seismicity/

for
Paul Vangelisti,
Douglas Messerli
&
in memory of
Leland Hickman

CONTENTS

The Hero Is Nothing   9

A World   27

Arena   45

Twenty Questions   81

Book of Hours   93

Credence   111

Study for the Ideal City   159

Sand   171

Studies in Fourteen Lines   217

Study for the Possibility of Hope   257

Author's Note   279

Afterword   281

THE HERO IS NOTHING

1985

Dream of Ocean (with Doors)

This dream riddled with doors at night
when you fall overboard no one hears you.
In the morning your scream has cooled and merged.

It would be up to you to float calmly, waiting,
or seek one of the doors
but then rescuers would find nothing
that would matter your choice more final
than their worst fears.

This dream is a hard test.
It is a dream where you say again and again
"This is not a dream. This is waking.
Only in waking can this be said."
You see a deep channel
and in the pulsing waters doors.

Trilogy from a Japanese Lullaby in a Music Box

I

That we are asleep and not duly asleep but hear this:
The test of bells ringing we measure acutely by whose ears
vibrate in the first light, in the minor key of first color.

Minor doesn't portend unimportance, only tone
and tone without reference: sadness without context.

The bells might be soft tines of music boxes the melody
a Japanese lullaby this time waking us.
Sad, simple minor.

That we are asleep (it doesn't matter) no reliable judgment meant
no Cartesian deduction adhered to. That. we. sleeping no
interference between the combinations we want to make.
Ears and eyes exchange functions. This becomes solid.
And it's solidity that we've sought
                                        to avoid by falling asleep.

That we, sleeping, bells, tines' chimes' song minor.
Melody not a given, nor rhyme. Melody only one condition
from an endless set. Not preferable perhaps
easier.

  Asleep if the couch, boat, vehicle rocks
  off each of the possible axes.
  Roll pitch yaw that one view of the one first color.
  Open (means awake.) View equals melody.

2
We end in a trailer and derelict means broken asphalt
encroaching sand, you, I, our faces tightened the heat
derelict.

Something brings panic. Something brings up vestigial hormones
the need to run and yet there's a quiet room, sheltered and locked,
paper on one side derelict scene on the other.

This new phase is lost. New belongings lost.

Inside, the broken talisman. Inside the sand noise we make
    grinds
rebounds from floor to wall. Hollow sound in, out
on lubricant of cleanliness and repair.

This new phrase, rude organizing.

Around the trailer sand on a fractured asphalt slab.
I suddenly become your enemy.

Something brings panic. Something brings panic so strong and
    stubborn
we get tired, or wait, it's me not you, you're in the trailer
I'm trying to get back in.

And dive down again down to the door
to the asphalt scarf.

We are asleep, no not asleep but gathered, not touching, in heat.

Why do we repeat this scene? We are safe not captive.
Why come back?
Not because it's pleasant. Not for reward.

3
If dream,

        disc, alarm
if things immobile if omens,
anniversaries, danger are dismissed
and if "and if" were fossilized, barracked along
rows and rows of beds?

   If only seeing part of you
   only isolated parts.

If they won't let you move freely only
slippery through them, if, "If 'if'" is only question not
proposition then.

Of you sinking. Then, if.

   If I wake from hot napping
   and the dream is too close to the fast blade
   and I see you for a second
   in the cloth of your danger, then.
   If.

If only seeing you.

History as a Moment of Patriarchy

Strata of cloudy liquid.
Williams hovers below which Williams you ask.

Light, imported (from where irrelevant) in tubes
to be used for sudden illumination under ledges
or between the positives of crevice.

A boy and his dog somewhere beyond Williams
in a protein too injurious to risk.

The light is used. A sound has been detected.
Proper procedure dictates special behavior which
is not feasible. Light is employed to search out the source.

Companion, rest stop, director, passive viewer,
passenger, bread mate, dark sonnet,
lemmings tail us we must be cautious.
Below are the presences of our past
a well we draw from but
an impulse to be thwarted impinges on us.

The obsession with seeing below to them
thrills us.

The light of the world is uncontained, filters down
through abstract layers
from an unquenchable constant explosion
onto the surfaces of porcelain or grey moorings;
is silver and even, falls like a blanket
ignorant of its past.

Landscape

This peculiar combination the
right streets wrong streets
tread (trepidation) lightly a
                yellow mar
          tarnishes forward momentum.

The landscape is a control.

          I'll hold you down because you're too buoyant because
          each time the scene I want you to notice comes by
          you're bobbing above it, out of view.

     A scuff of yellow. A mar
     on the well-tended surface.

If one stays away too long the membrane of landscape grows tough.
You say the bobbing from details is a stropping to keen you
to enblade you to lightly slice the membrane.

Membrane of landscape the apparent visual of where we are the
control of what happens not the control that events and things
are regulated but the control that things, events are measured this
control is only a backdrop, tempera paint and clever lighting;
all scaffolding that must be broken down if the next membrane
     true yellow
mar of your attention is to be placed are to be positioned.

          *

Only the passage or gesture.

                    Tank emptied the
          species spread out flat
                    suspension tossed.

As if breath taken deeply in and released in crescendo
were not the completed structure but the essential element.

          Water is another.
          The living things in it
          without it dead.
          Breath gone.
          Paradox to terrestrials.

Essential element the motor of death.

No vessels to pierce.

     Passage would not *mean* anything.

Three-Part Requiem

Somewhere an image comes clear I
recall the grains of wood thinking of this
driving rain but
can't come up with the scene.

Not Uncle Milton 48 hours dead, sitting in the cab of a pickup
    truck
already buried, eviscerated and still
on the road sitting white and straightforward
in the cab of this truck I
watch him hoping "Heavenly Car" but that scene too
is an island.

I rise. Cat vomit my own
incontinence dripping this scene
an island.

There are one-hundredfold reasons
called Heavenly Cars, called On the Road
to Islands, called What Drips.

I am sitting on the terminator
of a great umbra.
        My shoulder has tensed into cramp
        locking against my ear
    as if
    quoting this scene makes it real.

        *

Bloodless uncle fugit.
No guess, the arcane ology.
Taken along or left silent behind?
No reminder late
in a terminal portal
of how briefly the witnessing was permitted
or how sorrowful, forgotten, studied
the fragments.

    *

     Funeral.   Rain.
            Dim man pressed
     into earth.

Self-Portrait

You. Your attentions. What others say in empty halls
of no concern but where's your recompense. Do
they recall your fine manner or deft art in the conferences. Where
are you when these things happen?

So detailed attention to the effect of doors, rain, ocean
there *can* be a debate inside you.

Roughness and electrical affinity may mark your hovering what
else would concern you?

*

You rain-procuring mercenary whose *true* claim we disbelieve.
Dracaena stump expected to blossom tropical in a water jar
on your oak desk the structure of which
conjecture causes your anxiety to see a poor cat
legless, placed in a thimble, faced toward a window that
views fern forest, to wait and look as if you saw
some other significance in so pathetic a scene
as if it were ungenuine, too soft against the rock-hard
vision you seek and so include various hardware
and a backdrop or urbane holidays in tropical settings.

*

You ask why you can't simply make beautiful things the
world you're capable of invoking in itself is moving and then
you become restless and picture the wingbeats and accompaniment
of "Sunday Morning" and know the answer and settle again
for what you demanded or were handed or
what always comes up there's no way of ensuring a result
or a conversation later you'll probably not hear it
or the alternative (you fancy eaves dropping after death) of hearing
them talk about you would be in the context of a world that must
negate the thrill of being remembered.

*

If the picture of cord or rope comes into this it's with
a sense of release not bondage as though
the twisting structure of rope or cord were a pathway not
a prison and if Wittgenstein says that philosophy
must be as complex as the knots it seeks to unravel
then poetry must be a knot, beautiful and impossible
that instead of needing to be untangled,
of its own accord blooms.

We fall to the underworld by choice.
Smaller and smaller details beckon.
Their voices imagined, finite.
We cannot retrieve lost things.

But insoluble darkness
drinks light and sound and touch,
pulls us to its shore.

We arrive without offerings
for the voices awaiting blood.

We bring only heat
which rises back to overworld.

No voice greets us.
Nothing is received.

The Name of Polybus' Queen

Don't. In this glade. Beside a box we found
feign birth. We know the ruse.

Let's instead of the box
          open something softer:
Obsession is softer. Obsession conforms to all shapes and angles.
Suddenly obsession blanks the faces
nulls the voices, makes things hard
but sometimes numb.

Rumor has it that the box contained a child.

So take me to the white house.

In the white house we have discovered the secret cache
of rare wine we may not touch. We
have implanted ourselves in a small loft
because the half-moon light white walls
weaken to us.

A public demonstration only confuses matters.

My warning to you needless, I know. That *was*
you on the beach of river and ocean.
I did see you, didn't I, carefully pounding the box
into splinters, the name of your husband on each slat.

Your child is safe.

Elpenor reaches in, attached but vanquished.

Small amber cubes, sharp cubes clog his ears.
We borrow Elpenor today, we like him
partially deaf. We have no reason to give him
all he wants is a proper fire.
We borrow matches to console him.

The hero is nothing.

From limbo we are given a new vine
its leaves are furry, its casings burst
with orange flowers. They will burn completely
but only at the right moment, by the right corpse.

Then find it
barren as always.

A minuscule change, angle of light,
that's all. I would stop here.
I would stop and wait for recall.
Instead I salmon up this dry bed some
instinctual pool calling me but arid
I slap down on hot boulders, belly over, push
against air.

At the pool Persephone is laughing.
She opens a red fruit:
it's filled with fish eyes.
"You're here anyway," she says.

A WORLD
1989

He awoke in a crowd that stared
into a giant light or fire. No voice dismissed them.
No compacted or tilled soil detained them.

To find himself across a continent
surrounded by singles bars and convenience stores.

There had been troops but he escaped.
Down the steepest hills
from barren housing tracts
to overgrown truck farms
to where he couldn't be found
he fled.
His sister's last words "You'll be killed"
dropped behind.

Sad farewell to familiar scapes.

His gestures now his own among strangers.
A light or fire, a signal. "Notes," he says again.
"Only notes."

Europa seduced rides isleward.
Details cover her.

She would say to you that which
took away. Each word a minus.

Warm wind shrouds her arms
estival, noon, tired, calmed
a smooth moment where rough once was.

She would hold up a condom.
Remember her eyes?

Currents sweep in. A Crete we can't find
still sends its missives.
Her arms freed, even as the divine bovine
swims out to sea

the beautiful, reillusioned warm one astride.

And fog soft night harbinger summer soft
soft lips bare skin soft
season of fog precedes season of temperate nights
vernal to estival, specific
to the city of the ocean's plain

Worship at which shrine believing in none
but adoring the buildings and masks, ceremonial axes,
sharp ceremonial chairs

Came in a wave of sleepspeech
the body walking the brain heavy
in an ecstasy of sounds. Was the temple the goal
where only a wall remains
at midnight driven through the labyrinth
the ancient city in deep shadows, in sleep
to roll a tongue of paper
in a chink of stone wall

Request? Demand? Curse?
then running back through internal alleys and stepways

plain awash, acid droplets and base
young white fog
to arrive at a bastion
unlikely yet craved
and at the fences
drink the fog
cool and quenching

Found your island play
in time to be occupied elsewhere
in time for fogs that prove
new weather.

We said you were someone otherwise distracted
and held up a number of models to compare you to.
None worked which left us staggered in a desert
near a long runway we had built hoping you could fly.

You know the players
your pawns and rocky elements and barren
a place to seek vengeance
for a lifespark you claimed to taste
in this indelible fog.

An *Iliad* of protection the rules suspended
by whims and lusts

You waited in a Judean tent
held your black curls overhead
desert wind a shawl you wore

Black, red, mirror, gold

While the hero sulked the sperm surrounded
pecking and whipping, pecking and whipping

We as gods adore our flung components
watch and root with a new recombinant confidence

In that light the slight bow of your neck
tiny arrows embedded in the cloth of your blouse

Your bare thighs spread open enclosed in Judea

lips (care lesse lips to misse) apart
full lips a word no gesture
(gold to airy thinesse beate)

You issued complaints as protection
our red eye looks in on the action
pecking and whipping till none get in too
complimentary

Your pelvis the world
where this revolved.

Light gentle bow today a new curve
hot light glass trapped
decrease the glands' speed

your bare thighs strong parting
letters won't cure this
nor hashing over who will answer and who will not

only the tepid warning, never precise
never understood.

He waited to drain all adrenalin
and drink it from a tumbler.
There's the lightning. Where's the god?

You called your heart a flutter
not a beat recalled your
hand which touched its chest
but dug in harder or a gland
deep inside.

It wasn't violence
it was writing.

And "this" is an easy reference
contained, fragment
of a world.

Where the heart will be the whipping boy
the way a dream will speak in opposites

the way you might finger an adrenal
but it's innocent, just responding.

Water drips then sprinkles, showers down
a dark slab. Angles, double angles, triple
spring apart and light filters and wet jungle air
blankets you this morning removed but still wrestling.

Might have given you a retreat
but you and your "civilization."

On the floor where the goddess.

In the air.

Connective tissue yields a malady
or a membrane passage.

Her eyes sunken.

Or it was water
under pressure in pipes
timbres hummed
and you said
"Harmony" and said
"So sublime" then
"Lovely" but meant something
serious.

The house alive.

As: where she slept.

And where she slept all
symptoms matched up.

Things were touching:
Vibrations earned sound

the house a tuning fork.

The goddess slept on middle C
frequency, amplitude
timbre, decay

You said "Whose small mouth
did you attach?"

But this air.

Survey Surveillance

I

The shelf of rock
the layers of rock, rock ridges

The keeper we have watched
the keeper in green

Coat and pants

Read this in several months to people
who might be there

The top about to blow off
but the man in green
on the shelves of rock

Because adrenalin's electric,
shelves volcanic

2

Who came from his hut angled against
wind and rain. Horizontal world.

Tiny oven but electric. A crucible
and an eyecup full of molten metal.
An eggcup then if eyecups don't.

From where each day I'd observe him
dressed in green walking
from the neat lumber of his cottage
to the rough strata that feathered off
to a wet landing in the water.

No amount of adrenalin could.
Or any amount, so.

His record evidently by lantern light
until dawn. Ash leaf after ash leaf.
History? I wondered.

And named a name.
And was seen. And was stuck in a moment.

3

Dressed on fatigue. Layered in stone.
Confused between a taut musical line
and a plumb line. Lyric and narrative.

Layered in stone. On stone.

One temper or tempered line.
Annealed in steam and water.
Water then steam.

First he's static.

4
Only thought a motor held by thread
a backlashed head a day at Inca pyramids

then slap, fresh storms
strang water on black rock.

Dressed in fatigue.

Letters to the vanishing point.

No amount of adrenalin could.

If the day would be fine then.
Cold bodies plunge into ocean.

From where each day I'd.

Or from the next landing see him.

Persistence of memory.
As if he really moved or I.

We live in a city.
But this one has streets.

Layers. A sheen.
A dozen million assassins.

And a rain so acid
a mile later, a thousand miles later.

We drive on the streets
a thousand dry footings this time,
summer and incredibly
no one can remember which street.

Once there was a man like a wall
so tall so wide and now
a city. We live in a city.
That's us now. Housed in a mirror.
That's us looking.

<u>My Mosque</u>

Your sandy skin

a Moorish wall
beneath

or a general of Venice

The stark of rock and a
central plain devoid of orchards

a city of arches and Mosaic
Maimonides in full aphorism

Sunny and populous

a dim memory

start with title.

You call and the fabric collapses.

Faint expectation, please cheer me,
then plain, flat

missiles were shot again today
at first toward rumors then
the body of their leader was found.

Some deadly genetic construct is released
message from dying organ
to kill as much and more
win a bright spot

then silence, call dispatched
to plain tone, howls
dismissed, too weak, too strong.

It may be true that it's all about
amassing an audience that thinking beyond that
is only a decoy

or it may be that some fluid
chokes us off so sharply
only a decoy would save us.

They hold up dead daughters
then everyone hangs out their dead.

Nothing is solved.
Only the arena enlarges.

ARENA
1991

EXILE

But perfectly random and coastal.

A convention that forgot you.
People, whose names would be dropped.

Would it be an offense to approach them?
They sit there, each one, thinking things.
Eyes so focused. Mouths tight.

Your means of travel extraordinary,
private, even secret.

Or just physically, the restaurant dark,
large windows, south-facing,
overlooking a huge crescent bay; tables
full of families.

Where *any* phrase might come from.

Goddess slept on middle C.

Or a witness in olive drab.

Convocation of members, filial,
although outside the cars pass oblivious.

It would be so bright where they'd send us.

It was she (not it) who didn't come or if she did
it was a careful secret that only she could reveal and only
she controlled and if that's not abandonment then
maybe she *was* there and what I wore, just by accident,
was the uniform of the place so that no one would ask questions.

It was only my time.

When suddenly you slice open a belly
or cut off a hand.

A small discretion
an accent (target)

accepted compression

We counted laps and reports
trusts and comments,
fearful predators and benign ones.

Perfectly random and coastal.

And you sank into a noon
of expectation and history.

Not an annotated history or a homeland
of your displaced hero.

Time then acquaintance.

The dance more appealing without sound.

Light embedded in the devil's name.

A family gathers on hot nights
under a full moon.

If you were alone.

Light, generated not reflected.
Like heat, or lightning.

You hear voices. No weather to propose.
A fire in the distance.

Who gets to carbon first.

Footsteps filtered through parchment.

Conflict of possession.

A convention that forgets you.

And we who assemble. Packed goods carried in.
On shining trays. That oil is pressed
and used, drilled and pumped.

Or arteries which once did not know
and now know, or their brains
or their research.

This would be towns. Congregation.
Human intercourse but first
a person or family then
a bend of river or fertile plain.

And we who gather together.

That far away there'd be a farm. That many farms
and villages and towns and coitus and train tracks,
highways, jetways, shipping lanes, language.

Or a laboratory.
That once none of these now all of these.

Gathered together with faces.
Esteemed colleagues.
Many dozens. Silent spines.

And time, a factor. Time and acquaintance?
Or only time. Then acquaintance. Then
acquaintance and other factors.
History and culture.

A chart.

A captor who disappears
who reappears, who's beyond harm.

And morning because even dewiness can't yield directories,
no neighbors no signposts in other words even if I escaped.

His shudder, my fear, random and coastal, a prelude

But I *fell* asleep and the tunes
were comforting, sappy, despicable.

Or imagined how it would be without a brain stem.

So I fell asleep, dreamed of the o.e.d.

Those captives are shades not marbles.
Or in dreams they persuade you.

Only the difference encouraging.
The dance more appealing without sound.

In this neighborhood cars run static, alone.

"It's because your writing is 'crafty'"

Then they defoliate. Their greatest joy
until blocks and blocks are bare.

The foreground is shadowed by glimpses
populated by things that have been taken.

Phantom sensations. Lost contact.

The background here.

Or just this day. Where data.

Or he chose the long route because it followed the sea.
Perfectly random and coastal.
It must not be broken off: the ideas, the voices
that repeat as impression. Your moves. Then boredom.

Resolves into a fantasy of travel; of sojourn
in austere hotels, at the headwaters of historic rivers.
Not about popular culture and not not about it.

And counted how many would attend and how many wouldn't.
Saw the small cards and felt sorrow then elation.
Divided time into pitiful increments
where before the week was whole. The day
a tiny chip, adrift.

The mysterious date an entry
(who gets to carbon first)

sharp voices from muffled rooms
or do the walls cause it?

Only a rhythm. Not the voices but between them.
Phantom sensations. Lost contact.

Then your name. In other mouths.
Are they heat or light?
And when you don't hear them?

Your hero against burlap. Soundless, preserved.

And when they do? Tap out the meter.

These are three dimensions.
Different histories.

Thunder or aircraft.

This all toward clarity
modest, retaining mystery.

Or: tasks to consume time
when time wants to be prolonged.

The mystery must never be in the line.
It is winter. It is 1729.

INVASION

The new town was not predicted.
Was it a brothel or the usual clarity
of the winter sea?

If the revolution had come.
The sense of betrayal
and giving away the belongings, so final
so maybe there was no choice maybe
the vanquished one would understand.

Or there was only an empty room now
and the light was the same as it had been.
The windows still in position.
The paint, the floorboards.
A print had to be replaced or a rain-soaked wall.
A few messages had been left.

From the shore the water revealed
coral sand at the bottom and fish
collected in swarms and couples at the shore
were ready to leave it was late in the day
the blue clear green and the smell of their dryness
and no system would replace them or the water
but the right thing was only a favor or a burden
no others watched them and they weren't the ones to feel
these complaints.

I am writing this on an island in a turquoise ocean
the hurricane lamp is flickering in the tradewind my
daughter is sleeping and only the images.
Neither revenge nor magic.

*

The hunt among them had been cancelled.
Why would no one pay attention?
When you visit the author ask of her works.
The stomach for or against.

From wall to wall only light occupied the space.

Perhaps there is always one who serves a sacrificial role.

They may never pay attention.

The neighbors were oblivious and took all that was given.
The new town was not predicted.

Attention to detail: the brothel
was alluring but the public waited outside.

It was autumn. Cold and clear.

I am an old man stealing from others.
Neither magic nor revenge.

*

On the opening. Or press against me.
It is clear and the air is clear.

On. The. Opening.

Or maybe I can't stop.

The light of the hurricane lamp.
The island from where I write these memories.
The shipwreck that brought me here
and the shipwreck that rescues me.

The oak was burned evenly. The customers
were unaware that their first duty
had been replaced by a smoking machine.

You ask yourself whether your indifference
is sublimation or if you are simply indifferent.

The lines are stolen from a character
in the Alexandria Quartet. Or perhaps
from the Tempest. Or the lines survive a
colonist in Polynesia or the mythology there.

An Atlantic or Pacific island.
Mediterranean or Caribbean.

Resting or release point.

Under the acacia then no sun
the swell has shifted and we sail
on wave faces, sailed.

It is a taste a wall of silver
on a field of cobalt the caress
of depth.

Strike anywhere.

Granular night and the caress
of humidity.

The schools of trumpet fish and parrot fish
and surgeon fish that follow us
in a volcanic bowl.

The caress of tradewinds warm
at night.

The salt and then through a corridor of jungle
perfumed with rotting passion fruit
a dark pool, fresh, chilly
poured from a narrow falls.

A blue abyss, constellation of fish.

Sitting on the out crop
by the light of a burning daughter.
It is I in a fish scale
patched and nervous.

The sunset is hot
the eastern clouds black
the palms against them
ignited.

Light lost in the transition to summer.

The words at a party
story in a movie script.

Don't expect us to listen
we've been riveted by the hostess.

She forgives the way drillers have left her land.
Sonic booms lattice the sky.

An impasse and a summer air volume
the pressure passes lower then
a little lower. The remembered park,
The vindictiveness of disappointed love.
Pictured as a single point in history.
Any.

A shoal as in a reef a block
smaller than the incidents that make it and then humors
to see them in that context,
so confused so searching for connections
headed off at the pass.

She found a new place in a new land
and started a new life just like that.
Will the tapes arrive on time?
Is there tennis there?
If you fall from your balcony to the street below
will it be hard?

Tapering slowly. *Disappointed love.*
The servants will hear. They will invent
the stories to surround phrases.

There are fingers that would relax.
The grip is painful.
Some things cannot be discussed via rhetoric.
The table so crowded with timid faces.
And far away the *disappointment of vindictive love.*

We know the image
and they're not going to let you
say something.

Sleep will evade you
and we know the rules for interpreting the meanings
out of disconsolation.

Nothing can replace the sleep as if a moment
really could be recalled.

You thought this would be a period
of excitement and invention, a Swiss-style
chalet with devices you had only dreamed of
your balances confirmed on a moving slope of teflon
a frozen wave perpetually breaking.

I have pulled a string of cloth
over your hipbone
a thousand times.

Waking *and* writing.
You will speak of a certain presence
as if charisma were a misused term.

But you mean a person or spirit
that enters your thoughts or room.

I write this from my island cliff
a lantern on my table.

Someone who is not of my conception.

Entirely you will recant.

Fix this here. Fill the new canister.

We will remember those who suddenly disappeared.
It is no longer a secret. Those
histories are now too transparent.

What can we afford to spend?

Where a year ago.
Having come.   This far.
To make room
for a reader.

Or haunted
by birdsong
in the middle of the night.

Where these pieces.

Taking now what you might need later.
Or not knowing.

The daughter writing by lantern light
while I sleep, a mark on our island.

He turns over or bumps me.

I write: Good news cannot be accepted.

As if subterfuge were invisibility.

Though the wasp you slaughtered
buzzed until dawn.

And your insisting that the air was a shawl.

You had traveled on the thirteenth
after all the systems you disbelieve
again forsook you.

The idea that anyone ever sleeps the whole night
without waking.

Or that you might integrate all your reading
into your writing.

Though it will rain the air will be warm.

"No part of a different world will interrupt," you add,
knowing that the throes will continue until dawn.

And though a voice will likely answer you
or a temperature, or a viscous air

To begin with a caldera, underwater.
This in a breeze to keep the mosquitoes off.

The perfect fatigue fighting waves and currents
tides and neuroses.

Then an earthquake because
even or especially volcanic islands.

From which I write, the daughter who speaks to me
at dinner over lettuce, calls me to the railing
or there is no railing calls me
to an edge an outlook, over lettuce,
where we have come.

But whose daughter?

"I am ineluctably drawn to islands,"
I wrote but couldn't use. She said
"I'm drawn to you,"
but couldn't use "ineluctable."

What the gift would be
despite the convention's confusion.

The swell that travels across the Central Pacific
enters the bay and deposits a wad of rope
onto the shore.

Perhaps irises.

Where parrot fish nibble at the plinth of the island.

Because there is a voice of reason and a voice of control and a
voice of madness and a voice of sand and a voice of order and a
voice of forgetfulness and a voice of dryness and a voice of iron
and a voice of glazing and a voice of humidity and a voice of salt
and a voice of attachment and a voice of daughter and a voice of
father and a voice of the base of the opening of the remainder of
the form of the stuff of the idea of the island.

You should put the stamps in the stamp box.
But a black pearl is there.

Luckily there are no pictures.
They left before loading.
And now only chairs.

When finally a mourning dove.
And we opened the cask we'd been saving:
It was filled with cloth
or was made of cloth and filled with liquid.
We dressed then, or drank.

I have concluded that what they say about the ozone
is right. Summer is now overcast.
Doors open in succeeding houses, the lids
of trash cans are removed and replaced and somehow
I suspect the worst.

The dress I wore or drank to the ball
(was it a wake?) and it's compressions on my private parts.
The dress I lifted to show you.
We did it quickly (I came four times, you once)
we were late for the vote.

When finally the tide shifted.

Below us the bay and the ocean.

I know where you are when you're sleeping.
I found the letter you wrote.
I was relieved but alarmed.

No sun is left for this season.
I'll speak in generics whenever possible.

And every state will introduce itself
in calm Latinate expressions.

When finally the avenue.
The cask they sent to our room.
Every night an orchid on each pillow.
Rum from rain water.

The dream played on the ceiling above you.

Your dress so tight.
You lifted it and smiled.
The boat would leave but the launch was delayed.
You came ten times and I twice.
Or was it one and one or twelve and five?

We were gathered there that day.
In a cave we found an albacore.
We cut it open and removed the aluminum.
We placed it, one hand each, on the podium.
No one clapped but on the replay they did
and someone dabbed a tear.

I was going to smooth your hair.

There is a long line and the sun is too bright.
The letters that came burnt your fingers
and I'm just a witness without a name tag.

The conversation is about remote places.
Either the flowers arrived on time
or you have become only an idea
with no real place.

An ebb and a flow as in measurements of mood
or thought, as in expectation and now
put your shades on, the sunbursts will not respect
anyone's romantic desires.

On a day when similar things are said
and those who are now only ideas
conduct overt acts of healing for themselves.

I appear only to assure you that the use
of the first person is nothing any of us
need to hide from.

As if just finding the line would solve the geography.

By the light of the burning daughter.

In the shell of the rising hypothesis
tell us why the exile or who
the daughter.

In a vale by a cliff of a mountain
near a forest on the landmass
through the miracle of geology
to the passing lobes in the lasting brain.

There may not be such a place as an island.

We would not prosper there.
The ships that pass pass on the edge
where the play of horizons.

And we from our vantage.

She might arrive at waking if that line of words
would emerge. It's as though I saw them
and can remember their cadence.

Or when I sleep and she takes her shift
to watch the two horizons touch.
I've heard her then, but dared not look.

Those rollers across the ocean face
ripples from this height.
Arising in the shell of a guess
as if finding a line would solve her.

By her burning.

Or I the daughter, secret in plans.

The courts I will address or the tribunals.

From which shell I shall part the two snakes.
This light on this island.
My father awake in a lantern we grew.

It is a steel pin. Its color
across the vista.
 The shops would be closed if we could see them.
But they'd hold a passage if we were there.

Asleep by the cold lantern
he writes my voice
awake in my own fire
I create the world.

TWENTY QUESTIONS
1992

Four

Though the hieroglyphs were cogent, the message was disheartening; so much so that the decoders promised to confess ignorance and were seen as failures, but not for the right reasons.

In the mode of hysteria we would include both laughter and sexual hyperactivity, uncontrolled anxiety and the constant desire to eat.

Thus they gathered together each year in groups of 10 to 40 and professed truths to each other that were or were not enduring.

Being lowered into the crypt was not frightening until their feet touched the ground.

The equivalent was found in leaders of powerful countries who chose to invade other countries to solve temporary problems known only through surveys.

The woman at the party was concerned about the idea of lyricism.

The precision of their maps was of little use.

You may choose to sing but how the words are taken is never certain.

Some idea must lie behind such aberrant behavior, they thought.

Though the hieroglyphics were cogent the message was disheartening; so much so that although the decoders promised to return to work the next day, they were never heard from again.

It is a time of year; it is always a time of year.

It was so dark their lights were drunk up by the depths; no one could help them if the safety devices failed.

Perhaps the remnants of an ancient war.

Legalities were never an issue before the myth of democracy forced the invention of more elaborate lies.

They refused to operate, but then removed whatever they could.

Take / report / undertake / invade

Everyone they had known from a certain period of their pasts had been invited and most showed up.

Once at the bottom of the crypt it took them thirty-three days to discover where the "Written Wall" was.

Across the hall from the concert a small exhibition had been installed that cast an angle of interpretation on the music that could never have been imagined.

There was rarely a problem striking up an amusing conversation.

Nine

A clock must be bought.

Noticing the exact anniversary.

Then space.

The approach of warmer weather heralded by slower cars.

The policeman assigned to the case preferred to chat with the editor of a local Cuban magazine.

No single set of criteria.

Falling asleep would be easy and calm although lore of the region placed the sleeper at some jeopardy.

Perhaps there is always one who must appear dominant because of fear.

Facing west all day gives us an unreliable sense of how light in a region progresses.

That she was attractive to him seemed beside the point since he was too close to his own motives to see them.

When the workers arrive there seems to be an urgency in the air that might be traced to their employer's anxiety over money.

The earth has been striped with zones that attempt to remove the fluid nature of time and the spherical motion of space.

Looking aside, askance, looking indirectly, trying not to look, concentrating forward but remaining aware of the periphery are means of seeing the potential of dimensions beyond the usual four (five).

The darkness of the street may have been influenced by how far away from home it was.

Any set of regulations creates some disharmony.

When he awoke all of the appliances were gone.

Cubans living in the U.S. are not often the same as Cubans living in Cuba.

The boiling of water was a way of measuring the progression of light and shadow through the western windows.

Going just past the point.

Yet at night the ticking could not be heard despite the intense quiet of the area.

Fourteen

Pile all the dishes and make each person take one.

Gather at the foot of the landing strip and remove all clothing; wait for a plane to take off; wait for a plane to land; dig a square hole as deep as it is wide; bury the clothes.

Circle 12 times around the meadow, nine times around the house, circle six times from the entrance to the gate post, three times from the kitchen to the room, circle the circumference of the room 30 times, circle the center of the room 1,944 times.

Carry water up the steepest hill; place a living leaf on each of 30 flat stones arranged in a trapezoid; wait for the leaves to dry; while waiting eat only what comes into the circle created by observers who have come along; place one drop of water on each of the leaves.

Put pepper on a page, fold the page, open the shirt worn by someone of the opposite sex.

Find loam by digging for it; take a shovelful and spread it over the floor of the bedroom.

Each day for a year place an ounce of black bread on a field in the same spot; take gravel or sand from that spot each day; store the gravel or sand on the second shelf of a five-shelved bureau; each day return the gravel or sand gathered two days earlier to the spot from which it was taken.

Put the fork at the top side of the plate, the knife at the right side of the plate, the spoon at the bottom side of the plate, the napkin on the left side of the plate and exchange the fork with the knife, the knife with the spoon, the napkin with the fork, the fork with the napkin, the spoon with the knife, the napkin with the spoon, the fork with the knife; sprinkle crushed trilobite fossils over the plate, fork, knife, spoon and napkin.

Paint each fifth tree with a five inch equilateral triangle of the same color as the tree it is covering.

Sit in a chair in the corner of a room and pronounce silently the same word for fifteen minutes.

Open the blanket on the pile of earth; place a handful of earth in the center of the blanket; fold the blanket into a diamond shape; unfold the blanket; remove the earth and replace it with new earth; fold the blanket into a triangle; unfold the blanket; remove the earth and replace it with new earth; fold the blanket into a square; open the blanket and place a small log in the center; roll the blanket and log and earth into a tight cylinder.

Each day sit in front of a white piece of paper and, using a pen that will always have the same color ink, write upon the paper until it is covered with characters.

At the western-most extension of land collect a shell with at least one sharp edge; travel to a pine forest at the tree-line; define a rectangle 25 meters wide and 50 meters long; with the shell scrape gently at the bark of each tree within the rectangle; save whatever has been scraped from the trees using an eel skin pouch.

Learn and memorize the work for wink in every language and every dialect of every spoken language on earth; never speak any of the words.

Stare into the mirror at 11 a.m. and repeat your name 3,000 times.

Collect window putty from every glazier in Los Angeles, New York, London, Rome and Paris; place a speck of each sample onto a slated 2 × 2 card; place all the cards on the fifth shelf of a Louis XIV armoire, locking the outer door with a nickel-plated key.

At the end of every day for three decades, list each thing accomplished, no matter how small, during that day.

Invent a color code for the English Language; using the code, paint the Chapman translations of the *Iliad* and the *Odyssey* on the undersides off all the freeway overpasses in California; start over with the Iliad if necessary.

Place one inch squares of tape over all horizontal surfaces while maintaining an air of preoccupation.

Erase the word "the" from each departmental sign in the closest city with a population over one million; take a before and after photograph of each sign; shred each photo and soak the shreddings in a mixture of Pacific Ocean water, water from the Arno River, flour and epoxy cement; clear an acre of desert and dig, in the exact center, a twenty foot, capital, Gil Sans A; fill the A with the soaked shreds of the photos.

Twenty

The time was short.

On the first sunny afternoon in a month they dedicated then launched the new boat.

The way a palm shows its immediate history, or any tree in fact.

Voices could be heard from their hiding places.

Several stops needed to be made in preparation for this, the biggest festival of the year.

Back in their country where the average expectancy was so much less.

The sound of passing airplanes in the middle of a quiet day gave him a feeling of comfort that he could never understand.

Understanding that, among other things, hope and anticipation.

Whether through selfishness or guilt the neighbors had taken tremendous risks to save his life.

Several of the youth service organizations were sending representatives as a kind of gesture.

Even so, the field had been brown and fallow.

Of course, no one could promise good weather, but at least now, as they packed their bags, everything seemed to bode well.

She was saddened to find the field mouse, which she had been feeding, dead on the area rug.

At night, dressed in black, they felt able to recede into the shadows and remain undetected.

Given enough food and sufficient party favors.

It was true that in other regions seasons were marked through other signs.

The way that keeping a journal could be seen as preserving space and time.

Wasps, which had seemed to awaken with the heat, became lethargic in no relation to the humans near them.

Yet it was impossible for either of them to feel truly invisible.

They had been certain that Mr. Q had promised them the ball, so certain that they purchased new clothes and wrote letters to their relatives in cities far away.

BOOK OF HOURS
1996

No segment with the power to seduce
but the whole with the map of a villa.

Rain recolors the atrium.
Rain sluices through the roof channels.
Rain slicks the marble floors.

The bowl as a history.

The bowl as a history of a lake.
But now rain is the measure.

A dominant low pressure system
will gradually displace a weakening ridge of high pressure
over the basin
under the sparks.

The grievance is encrusted with only a trace of color.
We think of history as black and white.

Shelter is only a counterweight.
Cold air starves us to an ecstasy.

We touch the lip of ceramic tile.
We are told to drink from it
that once was a cup.

We forget to see the reason that cooked earth is crucial.
It is found well-preserved and almost ready
but now utility is exhibition.

Terra Cotta.

We're talking of saturation
and points of saturation.

Our picture of how we think the way things are
or should be,
our shopkeepers are sinister
they wait quietly,
a harp plays on their sound stage
their voices are mournful,
the problem of our belief is not an issue.

The argument could be the preface.
In the land of stone inscriptions.
Vacations and visitations conclude
somehow in synch with other rhythms
or a hundred things interface
shift and manipulate.

So quietly, as if volume determined virtue.
In fact the violence of a nation
also seemed quiet. But it was an herb garden.

The argument could work like an elegant and complex machine
and utility could not rest on its side.

Or the argument is architecture
towards which even liquid is ranged in
or maybe terra cotta
in the lives of saints
washing as it were.

The argument is architecture
with the structure of a gas

and the lining under the lining
and the figures depicting intercourse
on the sides of a *kylix*.

Because in a city the reasons are distant
and even the obvious need a certain disdain.

Where music is completely unknown.

We have found a new gravity.
The guards stop looking and their cameras are shut.
The back rooms are open and anything may happen.

The way narrative seeps in whenever the eyes close
or the pottery is reassembled rain is not narrative.

Sitting before the clock.
The argument has become silent.

The humming continues but we can't say from where.
You may look out at the green hillside
and enjoy the illusion of being away.

We can always find books in museum cases:
We enjoy the subtle light.

Before can also mean in front of.

Perhaps we find the more interesting part of history
to be in fragments.
Or does interesting mean palatable?
Proximity seems to yield narrative, but that can't be right.

In an age of obliquity, or has it always been oblique,
the direct are always apostates.

Somewhere in the background a drone continues.
Maybe it's mechanized; we hadn't thought of that.

In our argument of origins
and this would include families and reason

we have read in all the good books
passages we think we remember.

These are the days characterized as characterless.
As thieves are tested and trials extended.

Our argument vague, stopped somehow
by titles, by expectations, by the fear of origins.

The wailing in the background isn't human.
We relax our guard.

The conversation continues between rooms.
Fatigue is general but we hear singing.

We lie about being asleep
because we've got to move soon and certainly rain
lint and dust fill the air a terra cotta
Orpheus calm in his posture even minus his lyre
not as we supposed him
but now we have dampness to worry about
when almost every word has been used to serve the rulers
who despite their tricks for cleaning clean every surface
the powder remarkable in rain
but we fail at controlling activity
the ridges of pressure and troughs of pressure
even if we do sleep
our meteorology stuck in words and figures.

You will figure the location by a series of numbers
and the numbers will sometimes be missing
and the locations of the numbers will be diverse
and often the idea of numbers will cease to make sense
and the notion of location and the need to find.

It is the age of mediocrity and the pressure for ease
is powerful and insidious.

There are also those who would be relieved
to find just one unmarked fragment.

Dates become indispensable and latitudes
(which are measured in minutes).

We know that where things happen or are found.
And the idea of value which we create
and can't escape.

Or we dream of stationary cold fronts,
domes of high pressure, the influence
of jet streams and storm cells
which also leave maps.

In thinner air and by thinner
perhaps rarefied is meant: subject please:
a Caledonian passage, the script
of particular interest.

We pay attention to design. The languages are unknown.

Suddenly the weather is cold. Sudden
means we can also change our location.

There are manuscripts under glass
and tablature on parchment
where humidity's controlled
and the lighting subdued, indirect,
correctly balanced.

Stains from the calligrapher's spittle,
or so we imagine, have been filtered out.

Pulses race even at rest.
Insects don't need to be seen as aggressive.
The tiny wounds we accrued
have healed over and shine.

If something cannot be known, is it hidden?

But we disbelieve in ghosts.
The rumbling stops but we jump at the currents.

There was a beast whose scales were terra cotta.
We cannot offer what will be certainly declined.

And yet mention is made of persons or history
but something did happen.

Even the air will leave a trace,
somehow mist is recorded.

They who report on what seems to have happened
are no more present than their stories.

Nor is property a phantom.

If you listen, we know the way to make their drink,
the air, only their innermost fears are exposed,
sounds like water, our attempts to know them
have always been clumsy.

The air which feels like cloth.
The water which we know as a person.

We also know the phrase
after x he was never the same
and wonder at those who take so seriously
what to us seemed simply like music.

If, for example, the photographer leaves a camera
which the locals find
but they don't have film and never will
and who said they took it?
then any thing could be safe
and jeopardy a thing just sought for.

Or the phrase
In response to a cold front the ridge of high pressure

There is, after all, a thing called humidity
and there is, for example, Poseidon
or ignorance or the need for cause.

They have posed or been posed
and so maybe it's someone's fault or it's easy
to desire a system that begins with conclusions
or suggests a form, different each time.

Even if those icons are portable
and we mean cobalt roof tiles
we never know how another sees us
the atrium such a refined idea
or we forget ourselves
as forms may be invented at anyone's pleasure
winged victory could be housed there
we fear the wax or we over believe in combination
unaware how this may be seen
we mean a measure of thought
as if something always held out of reach
or we define worth by portability
thus the vanquished define themselves but not history
or we know not seems in the age of appearances
even if the most complex reasoning breaks down to rhythm.

But you would trade your warm winds
for the rains of December to walk
your airy atrium and remember initiation.

Nor wander in cloud cover
when the ocean mediates a harder season
something may lead outward but we wonder
how to escape and remain inside.

CREDENCE
1996

There would be dirt between the paving stones or at the nexus of stone steps.[1] There would be a painful coldness or the face pressed down in the gravel. There would be insects crawling on the bark of trees and we'll find out the species later. The first grains of snow on the concrete. Condensation on glasses as they're brought outdoors.

The stripe is not the same as who really walked in hoping to find action (a noun) or people willing to engage in something (probably sex) more stimulating than another deep conversation (standing in line) opened to a weather they cannot face.

The stripe being the emblem being the attachment being the texture.

Some items in the list have lost their appeal that is surface or sensation.

Items in the list may include the fountain pen or the paper it writes on, a numerator missing "3" in the second column, a chronology carefully rendered, an article of reportage thought lost but now discovered, we loved them once with all our hearts, the knowledge of anyone's location, any other thing they do together because it's what they always do.[2]

The name of action or stripe of action or an action will take place.[3] The only clarity. In a quartet the entire continent.

There is no way to measure a commodious vicus nor speak
here, when they command. The dream which she described. No
matter how many times we've heard that. I.e. at altitude the body
demands much more. Water for example.

Here in the shadow of a volcano. As in, we remember a written
scene which conjures up a certain stretch of road on a certain
island imagined a certain way, known to be different despite a
persistent image, wrong and secret.

Or they suffered in the illustration. A reflection of some weighty
concern. A real dissipation of migrations.

And yet – He saw the front of their house,[4] wasn't invited in, and
suffered in the illusion that maybe it was the road and yet he'd
always known.

Then commercials were raised as if we weren't surrounded. It was a custom to list purchases, a ritual to accumulate any thing collectable. Across these landscapes appeared a black rush which later was seen as people. A moment was therefore memorialized and turned into history. No matter how high they elevated the camera the view was never broad enough.

Though the population refused.[5]

Having successfully substituted animals for humans in most of their critical activities. Semen production, for example, was never as attractive an industry as it now was. This sudden shift, tempered by private desires, is what caused them to think twice.

Or picture the way an organism. Having successfully submitted plans for a genocide. But the whole genus. But we watched. A condom used as a demo. So incomplete. Their sentences. The intent.

Then you shall split the kingdom thrice. Messages will be left or
analyzed.

A comparison is made without concern for others' ages or aging
a component of how they thought or, besides you, have you ever
just jumped?

For the entire day the sourceless problem of having words which
begin p-r-o filling the brain.

Thus reductive, the squire, the contessa, the baron, the captain.
Their potency guaranteed, if not by salt and tobacco then we'll find
something else. Their depictions always so much smaller in the
paintings of saints and prophets.

They do not march but lead processions, i.e. corporal memories,
maximizing the piccolo parts, what they mean by change and then
a prolapse, bottom gone.

Thy kingdom thrice shivered to the bedrock. I.e. what you settle
for; a component.[9]

Thus they plaited bougainvillea no timbre unpredicated the
measure of a room compared to the measure of time.

Then one re-emerges and disappears and the concept of tracing
a conceit which is also archaeological.

Fronds which tap against each other as stiff twin compasses[11]
inscribe or whose notion of line or propriety or fossilization.

Ferns frame the windows of the invented room where a diph-
thong's difference is one landscape the visitors always surprised.

In a cobalt depth mid ocean. Petal, metal, who doesn't serve as reference. As reverence.[12] Phantoms pass below us. But how below? These ventages this governance. Interruptions. Eruptions. Thus the pelagic traveler. Or the littoral. What they must mean by replacing letters with words.

No matter how early or the word despondent[14] enters according to scientists who had already calculated the data.

No matter how many friends seemed to gather.

And thus we have the fragmented suggestive against the disconnected declarative. No matter how the light was described – as golden, as yellow-orange, as silver, as white, or the word crepuscule sounds like a knotted muscle or a sphincter.

The undeniable element of blue.

From any angle, they reported a finding.

What was it like or will be a memory, i.e. black and white, the background out of focus, presented cross-section, tempered, by numbers subdued, these compound verbs a tyrant, remembered by the people or will be,[16] full color then no color.

Measuring a forced issue, states broken down, a vocabulary, a human invention and yet measuring.

They might have considered other positions or opened[18] elsewhere.

Cornered and upbraided, a missionary among the just.

You may wish to have the case reviewed, and yet everything will be done to obstruct the information.

Persons of grave comportment rendered grave respect.

As this entire segment passes into a simple withholding of anecdote.

And yet the need for distortion.

They are entranced by a picture in blue light.
A grey morning when the surface is rolling.

Perhaps "era" has to do with offers and requests.

A grey moment in an age of specialists.

How shall the future catch up to the past?
The dimension will not be in grammar.

In an age of interference, even a thought,
where only a noise or a novice could.
Because only the specialist can.[19]

Or over a cloud say listen
a sharper notion than debate
tickles into concession these
terrible habits of dominion.

I.e. a platform constructed of thin stone
readied for a common interest.
Thus a popular cultural event[20]
open to the adventure of a winding road
honed to a razor's edge
or a cloud cover say or listen
the only idea he ever had annoyed him
or a cloud cover, bombed from behind
thus any head of state.

Having pushed a quantity of amber from the now much slower corpus, he set about with tasks which might have been considered gruesome, but to him were merely routine.

Where yesterday there had been a vista, today there was only a gloomy haze.

Resolution[25] was an entirely new issue.

They woke him, which to him seemed sudden.

So sudden. The cult talk resumed.

Though several swore the lake was ringed by mountains.

As they questioned us tremors[26] invaded their gestures.

These days on the lake. Or, as they'd have it, a too remote tone.

They render a brief taste of the life they've preserved for themselves.

Though the interviewer never stopped talking and their really heart-felt need to demonstrate.

This had been displayed to him at an earlier time in his life when only a rhythm[29] had seemed worthy of pursuing, a matchless time he remembered by committing certain taboos but never with others.

Predominately they entered ready with one theory and yet how anything might be received thus accountability seemed either more acute as an overriding preoccupation or unimportant as a compensatory reaction.

Her feet, bound by straw.

Vide: several samples, left by passers, not so amazingly helpful, as if precognition, rusted ordnance, a copper tube, synchronous, comely, in Petri dishes or folders, a neat kind of process, here then, as they happened, all of them.

And not just objects but behavior. Thus the isolation most preferred and yet most also congregated.

Small vessels, so potent, conveyance, that is, motivation, conduit, in *that* world.

Then one evasive subject, vespertine, habitual patterns, or is that more grammar, yet there they all were, having also been there before, i.e. none of them were surprised by what they saw, remembered, and yet disappointment too, i.e. expectation, having been there before, finding differences, variations.

Drawing from an image that couldn't have come from the outside.

Preferring the liquid form, or so they informed the dispenser. Thus dark and cold, as suited for napping as work.

Religion, per se, was not even a question. Ambient air, they who had gathered, aromas, postures, procedures. The atmospherics of the place, or looking outward. Any congregation.[30]

The notion of metonym[31] was absent from the minds of the marketers who devised adhesive price tags which could not be removed. Innumerable commodities became the simultaneous declaration of their purpose and value.

Opening out, as in a sweater removed. A temptation to a seduction[32] and yet humor.

A grey sweater then.

Disruption of glacial paths had been the key to an argument. And yet among certain colleagues. That is, a restaurant or a forum for such debate. And behind the scenes. The procedure. Hence perseverance. They had visited the factory and seen the effect. And yet even that is anthropomorphizing. Though surely this far from civilization the ringing of a bell, especially a rapid ringing.

Or the alluring texture of lamb's wool on human skin.

Or even at the center of an historical movement. And yet the wind so unrelenting. Silent, as in human noise. As if the whole story had been believed. Thus acquaintanceship. Apollonian or the kind with no memory.

As the piano presented the first row of problems, so the road there was also emergent. But he stood at the front door, waiting to see their faces as they approached. His prolepsis.

Significantly, even though the handwriting sample was difficult, scales and spectra were employed. Ciphers even in the background. Where else could they expect to arrive.

Was it rhythm or melody,[34] both so engaging from the outside both so present, this in a laboratory a voice or word, the demand of context, overcodes, secret handshakes, toes in alignment, a comment shared by only a few.

A field comes before them. A general melody then. Refraction. As the bay bends, as waves deflect, or sound, or light, or marks. Inland.

Opened in a dry netted dazzle
or as the light shifts
and wind, thorns also new,
tempestuous or polar, prelingual or landed,
just prose-like, a remedy.

Then cutting, as in across, a curt answer, standing attentively or
sentries, overt in costume, cunning in exile, press this one point,[35]
the syllable which makes the season, though current shifts and
temperature and fauna.

Warm air will float on cold air and fresh air will float on salt air
and particles finally will settle and displacement and convection
or is that water.

Webbed a rhetorical gesture
insight, deduction
though continental
(area squared)
piquant though remonstrative
borrowed, rest,
measured
pro, de, in, re, con

For hours the boil was figured bass a comfort they sought to
quantify, some words banned too coarse thence a cool cupboard,
confused between P and B, that frontal, excuses, exhausted, seduc-
tion, proceeds.

Because a certain rhythm so insistent, a comma, inserted but still a rhythm thus shunted decisions were made, this place a vortex or tinted, what they call alba, insinuated, appropriate by necessity.

Political discussions disallowed, hence the liquid quality of flame.

His governorship had been granted somewhat as a surprise. Having quickly packed his diplomatic gear in a trusty sea chest, the remaining tasks had to do with sorting, something a botanist understands at a fundamental level. His eighteen volume study of the mustard family was shaping up to be definitive. Now he could assume the bishopric with a clear conscience. Yet there remained an area of further study, and as a woman of great erudition, she knew that the theoretical world of economics was ignoring certain real effects that she knew must be acknowledged. So she packed her diplomatic pouch and handcuffed it to her left wrist, avoiding the temptation to think of it as her ankle, those endless anatomy classes back in medical school still playing little games with her, although, to be sure, she never told a patient that they had a severe eye infection when she meant to say that the structural hazards of the overpasses were as extreme as the emptiness of the politicians' promises to repair them. It wasn't that she was married to someone else so much as it was his seemingly uneven apportionment of time.[36]

Prestige has nothing to do with it.

The very principle of waiting, the very idea of saving things.

We all know the accuracy of our own internal clocks, waking up at the same time each day, for example.

And so nothing could interrupt its continuous operation. A taste as if pennies in their mouths. Only boat fare, only a ride on the ferry.

Yes, he had encountered a number of specters. Anger was his primary reaction. My[37] our your dilemma. Was it a movie: armored troops (probably Persian), the sacrifice of virgins (probably women). Or did he face them. Just getting the names right.

Therefore all things would be treated evenly, that is to say, fairly. No list of names or behaviors.

The rain was brief but its brevity did nothing to displace the surprise. She asked, and not meaning to be funny, what it means when ancient (that was her word) Hollywood stars appear in one's dreams. Therefore all things would be treated evenly. After all, what ferry had shuttled you there?

Thus all this talk of outside versus inside. We were the bearers, copper on our tongues, and so they had no choice but to wait. Lists or if not lists catalogues, and how they might differ and what they are versus, let's say, stories.

Anticipation. Interim ideas. Nothing could or would interrupt the continuous operation. Even the food was gone, thus animals, foraging, had entered, probably after darkness.

They who comport themselves with a superior attitude.[38]

In an emergency situation, example: late at night, dark road, no one near, a century earlier, distant preparations, a war, a decade later, a prologue.

Heavy rain, the single porch light, a column, heavy seas, throw her a buoy! Viability.

A little bell seems to sound, dawn again, a series of rhetorical terms unfurls, and yet the breeze is slack, paper vessels are brought outdoors. Some remake ambitious plans while others bury jeopardy. Lost in a hallway of citations. Imagine it this way. Imagine a rampart made of words.[39]

Control is not an emergency. Birch trees, for example, appear in bright moonlight. That group of wanderers, ghostly or there's an explanation for it, preparing as we speak.

A week before, but where, i.e. continental drift, a misunderstanding of options (their vocabulary), lost in the forest. In an endless building, in an amphitheater, on a dark road. A bell sounds, or something sounds. Then there *was* someone. A year from now or this is a year from now.

Even the armed response failed to alarm them. The itinerary failed
to hold.

Only the periphery then. A failed magic. Instead, a physical
hunger. Confluence of densities. Strata of densities.

"I'm allowed to do it differently," her protest. Hypnosis cannot
be used as excuse or solution, others said. Misguided were the
attempts to please her or please any of them. A report called for
the precipitous. Too hot to be water.

Thus his dissensions, uncontrolled and uncontrollable, racked
the assembly, angered them, this otherness problem, their entrap-
ment, his calm in the face of acuity.

A layer settled. A physical hunger. A let's do that one again. Air
clear sheets clear. A correspondence interrupted, as if the pres-
ence of respondents, no matter how serious. Thus dedication,[40]
although the strongest of them seemed idle. An exchange, convec-
tion, transferral, heat to heat, tension to mercury, patina to copper.
A physical, a concupiscence.

At the edges, something moves. They take it but can't identify. A
copy, then, a reproduction. This then nothing. An equilibrium.

Thus as surely as he had been sitting there. The memory of a gathering precisely because the air was so unstable. The romance of exile. The line of thunder cells waiting off shore.

They were always making practice chemical decisions and knew any number of combinations. No matter what the news was. He felt a certain tightening in his scrotum and this was a good thing.

Even from the window they could see the deciduous plants. Yes, it was spring. Everything was opening, she remarked. The tops were like umbrellas. Some, she, too, felt.

But nothing could be proved. As if evasion[41] were adhesive, proximity may have been an issue.

There had been a confusion between certain liberal views expressed and the idea that permission for a transgression had been given.

How delicate: for instance, was it a strategy or just a comment, the enlisting of help or approval or attention.

The activity was generous,[43] which is to say plentiful. The frame frenetic movement. And there will be those, inside, who are unpredictable or unreliable.

The sudden inclusion of catastrophic scenes.

This is the seasonal experience. Existing outside the scope of any extant theory. Or is it sensual. Even refusing to re-read an epic novel, preferring the memories of it including the distortions and inventions.

Or a world where volition is created by others.

Having been hypnotized at the outset by music or having allowed herself to be. That which seems to be a confluence. And without advice and who asked for it. Because "back home" there was more than routine. Carried forward.

As thoughts become discursive, that is expository. We all agree (don't we?) that we can't know anyone's perception and that includes animals'.

Having arrived at a hidden world.[44] Hypnotized by music. And yet something was familiar. But the beginning was exciting. Which can feel like fear, arousal, nervousness. The caption is everything.

Then why not just list the words or even better why not just show the dictionary.

We might actually trade what for a strong dose of melody?

A surrender, a finale, a giving over to excision.

So the child sings out high above lake Balaton and I drop like a stone or a sea bird and you say the water's not that cold and we watch him from our plane the judge the distance the surface.

They can sew up the stocking and sew up the knee. A dark grey screen filters our view. The machine that records this limits our field. This would be a matter of attitude: Debris[45] commands us but then so does the view; not a distraction but an extract. They avert their eyes or refuse to speak, the murmur becomes currency, the tick becomes language. The old dogmas so unsubtle using words. Yet somehow the tone is set. They might listen, or so the rumor goes. But listen against absence.

All the noise all the paper. What could they mean by cease and desist? Demarcations would please them. Zones could be decided and enforced. Each perimeter. Each command. A protocol.

The bowl of rice. Staying in constant voice.
A continuation.

For some masker has painted here.
A cobalt or a carbon.

There is an attitude and that's location.

There will always be the sound of engines: hollow and distant.
Part of a strategy.[46]

Who opined once without a message, or this was the legend, the map.

What they projected, hence, everyone had to wait, reconfigure, hesitate: a good sign.

There were a number of recorded responses, and a brochure. What selection if any. And of those who chose to select.

Hence nothing was said or something was burning.

The work of the west on us or so they would have us believe.

Credence.[48]

1   Where the stains will leave archetypes;
a correspondence then a vapor trail.

When to give up and when to turn process expository.
The eyes that persuade you will have no bearing.

The slogans will seem flat.
There are no stories.[a]

An idea of light on a desert basin's floor.

2   It is late.
Long-necked airplanes reach through velocity.[b]

Close your eyes. Hollertalk of drunkens.

3   It's only forensicc if they find the pieces.

4   They are entranced by a picture in blue light.
A grey morning when the surface is rolling.

Perhaps an era is defined by offers and requests.[d]

A grey moment in an age of specialists.

How will the future catch up to the past?
The conversion will not be in grammar.

In an age of interference, even a thought,
where only a noise or a novice could.
Because only the specialist can.

5   As the restaurant turns around a story
    ten convicted, Morocco, yes the daytime, older,
    pulse-ruled.[e]

    Were the messages complete?
    An open mirror might disrupt the sleeping students.

    As the world on axes erupts.

    Shown as an underwater cinder cone
    sounds emanating as the world on pinpoints.
    Imagine a processor, blank but efficient.

    The room, told a continent away and a decade.
    These are the traps: Only notes left behind –
    suppressed then hunted,
    interpreted as alibi, secret in plans.

9   They call for smoke the drop the poison the blank file.

    Ask for the easy pen.
    Decomposition is rampant.

    A process, the meaning of which,[i]
    your tactile anchor, the feeling of which.
    Not the Coral Sea but the Sargasso Sea.

    Nor the time nor the amount.

    The way the darkness in a dark room has grain but also motion.

    Or then sounds that carry some irrational promise.

    A message in the form of acids
    dripped in sequence on copper or lead.

11   Tangle in bars of light.
     A correspondence.

     Particulate.

     The vines then telluric,[k]
     indisputably over with.

     The indicative birds
     awake although dawn is frozen closed.

     Tell them it's only lessons.

     Residue filters through dormant vines.

     Tell them it's rehearsal.

12   If there were a different machine but there's not.
     Debris is skimmed away.

     On a concrete slab something pours,
     the sound of hardware down a walk way,
     the cold cement, the molecules, atoms gelid,
     the break as it crashes, just a squeak,
     no other signal.

     The random drumming.

     Dredging the pieces in their history.
     Dust so fine it's almost fluid.

     Then steps release a noise of pipes,
     a drone of vacuum, the dragging of dullbottomed[l] barrels,
     the wheeling of light loads.

14 Then I collected rents
    and only I could understand them.

    So misty when I'm gone.

    These properties of attachment.

    I said the ground or ash.
    I said the fishing rod or the special knife.
    I said weak as a cat
    or predict me a finish.

    What they'll say to my son.

    A hurricane churning on the meridians[n]
    spiral hours, index time.

16 A boy in the tree of the wolves.

    A type of metal fatigue:
    you can *smell* the ink.

    It is not diplomatic[p]
    to so ostentatiously hold court.

    We can see very clearly from the water.
    My bridges are far apart:
    My gun metal gray.
    Ice floating or cars.

18 The rebellion could be logical
    and the image they'd replace the icons with
    would only be a symbol this time.

    No matter how they write their parts
    nothing gives them credence.

Remove only a mirror and they turn blind.

What they forbid in their religions
they install in their states.

Burn them in effigy just to make a point.[r]

They wish sincerely to worship.

19 You may ask for quiet but the act becomes political.

If the light is blue the waves will be alpha.
If the noise is absent the pestilence.

Solitude is one thing.

Thinking faster than escape will allow.
City of specials;[s] our approval, our revulsion,
our rejected sinecure.

The day before you get there.
They can talk forever if nothing interferes.

In a world of novices.

20 What if order was restored?
Only standing in the shade[t] reduced their feelings of despair.

This is only a report, they were told
across their field of vision.

An aroma only at night.

25   Or another couple birthing with leisure.
     A voice is observing only slightly confused.[y]

     Shell is pulverized to manufacture a supplement.
     The parts are only a composite.

     That there shall be no restraint.
     It's as if a fiction, a visitation,
     a polar event with no workable center.

26   No doubt impersonal[z] reference was the central idea.

     No matter how cold at night the forest of music reached out with
     godly parsimony.

     A feeling that at any moment someone familiar.

     The hand of the dealers.

29   Just the simian remnants

     Occurred to me to undress
     or run.[cc]

     This precision.

     The smoke they release in the bathrooms
     and the magazines left in the street.
     It is a heatwave where their possessions ignite.

     Wondering who lasted
     the birds won't cease

30 The rhythm of inquiries trying to sound a tone
    i.e. what did you mean by sound?

    Banking on a characteristic turn of phrase[dd]
    rejecting a familiarity replaced with nothing.

    But who could expect such momentum? Even the most altruistic
    fall victim to an atavic urge for safety.

    How to compare discourse with intercourse.

31 Having traveled all night.

    A stranger who would not speak.[ee]

    Having come to a place where water and sky.

    Maybe tired. A colonnade just for you.

32 All agree that ointment is an uncomfortable word.

    You are tasted in the remotest spots.

    It was there, on the palmlined road,
    accommodations and then openings,
    the dust, the unbaffled light.

    Entering the time zone has meant nothing.[ff]

    If anointed the many women.

34 Whose momentary lapse, a meteorology of fact.
In repose, then. Diversity praised.

This is not a drill.[hh]

The bay so green almost luminous.
And they are so imperious (communal mode)
politic (momentary lapse)
stratified (structural summary),
though memory itself a chemical.

35 Or the word abeyance alone.

In a line just pretending in a circle.

Open horizons but motion
lined up or just tracking a progress.
Held in the arms then.[ii]

Trying to manage things causing complications.
Held his breath. Politics.

36 The order or the listing
or the delivery or the results
or a jungle of pronouns[jj]
or the expression
breaking the ice.
The implications
the confusion
the geography
the tail swung around
the sun
cold chokelessness
a billion miles
less than instinct
comet.

37 As if I could have visited a crescendo
    or subscribed to a mode of address
    uncommon to L.

    Yet – is there time to do this seriously? –
    from a distant room, through porous walls,
    commercial drama; i.e. approval was everywhere.

    A localized pain, no matter exactly where,[kk]
    reactivates an alphabet of persons.

    To think differently now.
    O's subscriptions are diverse.
    We had only responded but not posited.

    Yet even the vocabulary of explanation.

    The tone of endless supply.

38 Just because space exists.[ll]

    Although a discourse on physics would include the idea of
    attraction.

    Then separated.

    An opinion. A procedure.

    Although they valued anonymity, they always took the walkway
    with the better view.

39 They reminded and shifted.
    A gull-colored table with dignitaries.
    Trying will equal a test of will.

    In a form[mm] reminiscent of a time.
    In a song reminiscent of a smell.

Trying will equal a test of will.
They reminded and shifted.
A gull-colored table.

40 While what is known or any elemental fact

    absent a sense of romantic chiasmus[nn]
    or earthquakes exemplary of cellular resonance.

    If they had turned off the sound
    having left time and space
    knowing that even while traveling.

41 The way it would be at the coast, he thought inland.
    The power of remembering an aroma.[oo]
    There are certain adjectives that novelists use.

    She may have taken the fibre sample
    polite in her probation.

    The cold itself an envelope.

43 Someone says "Open your minds!
    Can't you see what you're doing?"

    As in a spy novel the word "and" is found on a pillow
    written in cold cream.

    Dozens of hungry customers.

    Will they wait with patience
    or will they rise up?

    Which one will wear the mask?[qq]
    Which will speak while the others decode the pillow?

Standing here we can't tell who has brought the keys
and who has hidden the foodstuff.

44 Through subversion.
    Telephone versus distempers
    (whispers furrowing halls)[rr]
    just ideas.
    The sleep of the just.

    Only a temper
    rightly adjusted
    this only overture
    a forward
    wrinkling a construct
    turning time
    across a field
    stars and orbs.

45 Their opals their concision
    reversed opinions railing against revision
    pure of invention amoral in tone.[ss]

46 Light divided past trees
    ground encircled.

    An opening on every page
    a series of figures complete then revised
    a persistence of thievery
    the arena of gambits[tt]

    foiled into elements
    can't take stock.

    Whose pen it is.

48 You may know how, the heart is unexpected
the heavy cover trapping

Or a process, part of a rite

You who would start something

The hangover of permission
like readmitting a word to a moving vocabulary

A first autumn
clarity and tinted air
the dropping temperance of water

They who disbelieve in seasons.[vv]

a. A wind-borne, avian winter.

b. To wish one's purchase.

c. The noise of a village, but a wind shift.

d. Here's the prologue let's pitchpole.

e. Is it the plain knowledge of an unencumbered self analyst or the blind residue of an age too attached to something it calls science or logic?

i. This is not the fulfilling of a program.

k. The vessel, the shadow of the vessel, the shadow alone.

l. Rather than concourse, a pavingstone.

n. Humidity too, a sudden voice out of sleep.

p. We were pure. Panic can be suppressed.

r. You have been consistently surprised by the retention of others.

s. The sudden quiet imposed by utility can attract as well as repel.

t. A shadowless suburbscape, a dry air, a tinted air.

y. We have listened they claimed.

z. As if a preceding power had transformed them to horses.

cc. Taken as an illusion then, would that work?

dd. Harmonically or atonally and these are the ones.

ee. Light beaded at the structure's chines.

ff. The idea of "It seems as if it were yesterday" really means clarity.

hh. This is not a theory.

ii. Their only horizon an air pocket.

jj. It is not liquid.

kk. By waiting or did they say wishing.

ll. Excited by the tardy, enthralled by the oblivious.

mm. Troops, someone said.

nn. Because there is no context.

oo. Others say that the sun had grown too hot.

qq. Nothing could keep a silence but this happens automatically.

rr. Was it you speaking to your twin?

ss. In the shade of a stiff wind.

tt. Rather than acknowledge a "through line."

vv. The sheets are clean. The oven announces us.

STUDY FOR THE IDEAL CITY
1999

Pescallo

They were only i.e. reflectors (glacial basin)
over a fixed number of kilometers (this region)

Said chiuso though the other roads ended in water.
Preview; we asked; some reason to work;
a temporal thing.

But on a ladder in tight tight pants
her garden oblivious, these pulse beats beyond the wall.

The heights, aristocrats' dominion, always in sight.

The boat they found without a bottom, a way to please her.

Study for the Ideal City

It is the attitude of the proprietors or the atmosphere.
At this point without upsetting the order of things
the dead may appear at random.

The idea that a very deep voice is protective.

You recognize the name which still appears on the machine.
A hunger for the subjective, too.

Instead of money (moneta) things (mementos).
From the machine, that is.

Each entrance taken with expectation. Routine.

    *

Implements of transfer then: coffee pots, automated teller
    machines,
telephones, letters, money, photographs, blank checks, bills,
    coitus,
speech, books, markets, motorized transport, chafing dishes,
an agent with one wrist hand-cuffed, wind.

As if an introduction. Yet that's how they got in.

The dead may thus appear, seemingly living.
No one else can tell the difference.

Her name on the machine
a proof that she had been there.

    *

Reduced to a question of payment.

The slightest doubt seemed a tempest of chaos:
"Never again, this must be controlled"
seemed their failure of analysis.

Which is not the same as a sudden disgorgement.

The owner was much taller; fear of public spectacle.
Or that function of service, a hierarchy ignored.

The owner of the machine was not traceable.
We stood in line and this was not so bad.

        *

That depth is a good thing, a desirable.
And thus the basso, so assuring.

Particularly in a restaurant, where a supply of coffee
or an ambiance, therefore a disruption.

The way some called "selva oscura" a metaphor.

Her name on the machine, that recent.

A turn at a certain pronunciation.
I.e. they really don't care, the locals, i.e.

Curious, to have omitted or forgotten streets.

        *

But simply the name of a painter named after a town.
So an emergence of a certain blue not otherwise seen.
And yes, therefore, a promontory and no
we would leave without begrudging the scholarship.

This isolation a biological trick.
You might like to call them vestments
in consideration of a specific climate.

Or a river named for a tone.

Would you call prediction order or chaos?

*

That sleep itself isn't a language.
Thus every seduction carries a new set of dilemmas.

Once gathered together there actually wasn't too much,
it may have been the process or simply the noise.

But then any idea of duration.

What the machine gave out instead of money.

Her name but not only *her* name, so any single clue.

You may or may not have an expectation.
A carrier, a courier, or outside, transport.

Desire

Or so told, a surface which collects light,
first image upside down, a pattern we've heard,
a feeling of exaltation.

Thus immanent, not to say without fear.

Enter she who would untangle the synthesis.

For example they who use "posit."

Then why make such a thing twice?

There was a danger
but we didn't mean that kind of immanence.

Kamuela

The difference was simply the re-emergence of music.

No matter that the reaction was physical, at least mentally.
As someone called it, the sticking place.
But then volume, not quantity.

Indigenous or did we mean colonial
or did we mean a kind of atavism.

Precisely because the voice
as in the interval between bouts.
And there's the operative word; interval.

Hawi

It is precisely the language of law though appointments
or predictions are matters aside.

Every house a kind of lookout or sentry post
because isolation or that's why they came there.

It was not an "undo" risk, yet many lines
seemed to have innuendoes that may only have been imagined.

Even by silhouette it was clearly heading southeast.

There always seemed to be enough air.

Her appearance was less a surprise than technically impossible.

Wind Line

They were each silent
while the windows moaned.

The moon fades out before it's passed, or so they observed.

As usual she was holding the key and kept it.

Or because the whole house trembled.
The glass itself a rare commodity.
As if anything for sale.

A new kind of insect was seen
and a response to any of the unsensed forces.

The Land Curve

Any eye, thus air. A pigment.
White caps calming. Precisely why we asked you.

Or voice. Any voice. Something to eat.
The long night spent.

Between or among.

The retina may remember but that would be scar tissue.
The phone rang, rings. A hidden coastline.

Money once seemed so important.
Even now, dust from the volcano, time zones, tiaras.

Fish Out of Water

The zero may not have been invented in the desert.
It is the pull of the moon, specific and precise
which leads fluids. Glass or sand, for example.

"Punctuality," it has been said "is closer
to the field of genetics than one might think."
Nor is specie identification unique to humans.

Not a development but a cornering.
Glass the invention of an island people.
Shop-keepers found mid succession, metals led.

SAND

2002

COMMITTEE WORK

Nor thralled by magnitude (depth or horizon)
nor tumid in speed (sexual reference preferred)
but thralled and tumid on a hump of fluid
in the clear single lighting of an examined thing.

Because time is the factor they grant
we shall not simper before the kegs they possess
an indigo light fusing equal memories.

Had the answer been insufficient the corps might wither,
the multitude might weaken, the instructions' gravity
commands co-operation "if only we could bottle it."
Faces lit in the light of their exchange.

In this world the elect are pristine.

The soft face
under whose force she
revised as in yet another pronunciation.

Her story then.

The house was full. No calls nor deep
nor long employed without paper.
This is how they enforce their codicils.

Imply a tension.
Or a shade implied by umbrage taken.

It is raining on the peninsula and dark.

You said you lived there.

When the floods came even the routine was interrupted.

I remember crying, even for the memory of a melody
he told her.

Each promise or statement equals a temptation
and yet holding to a story can often create history.

You said they still were angry.
This was more about alignment.
They are the note-writers we never see.

The way sitting down is internal
or hoping for a nod
separates a desire for cunning
from the cobbling sound of stones
tumbled in waters shocked

It's too early now
in the landscape or town you picture
the very idea of sequence is something you can't compass.

The way they place you on a deck
and all the types of things they call decks.

"My God!" they are likely to have ejaculated or said.
Their gift suddenly sours.
We know that separate worlds remain separate.

It's the zero which stares so hard
and not because we gravitate to the obvious.

They will miss you in the select committee.

Though volume would be a feeble measure
or the life of someone less real.

We pay because we think we must.

We wait for a tide held up by surface tension.

Fish swim above our landfall.

FIXED PHOTOGRAPHS

Someone called a period of wandering dreamtime.

These are the photos we save
on which the dead are fixed.

Against a black background.

In this dull city.

The revelations, though, would bring life to any place.
Or sleep, more a narcotic at this level of reversal.

So the voices that seem to originate from objects in a room
hurry here, the way things hurry
toward a background made only of motion.

No detail exempts us. But every detail is a trap.

Please don't imagine anything global.

The carp emerge at feeding time
and look through dangerous film
for the keeper.

These are not the times we waited and planned for.
The carp are often disappointed.

Your face but your location but your phrases.
Do we open the gate to enter
or because we love the feeling of cold metal on our hands?

The carp are called koi. We feed them from packets.

You can only hold up one end of history's expectation.
Time goes too slowly, too quickly, disappears.
No detail is forgotten.

We would from a quarter listening
to a new city beholden wake.
Only a debt could spin such gravity
and yet now only names revolve
empty of objects.

There is no postcard to relieve you.

But the ceiling's sagging under the weight
of an archaic snowstorm. The dune eats at the wind
and wakes you tired then cold.

The icicles cannot be tuned as stalactites can.

In one prone photo too saturated with color
too far gone to help now
accuser and salvation switch quarters
atom by atom.

If you give credence to one of the voices.

The madness of a winter of only five days.

If the moment is really all we have.

The adhesions we are helpless to.

As a cup lifts or a starboard signal
your face in the face of a specific nocturne
but the sounding is faint or vessel uncertain.

You forget the limitations of space.

Distance becomes a kind of future.

Although she wanted more than anything
just to fall asleep.

Someone had said it was merely facing the
blank canvass, or was that a sheet?

Only a beach two thousand miles away would suffice.

Worrying about the idea of place can seem to others
a disconnected activity.

However she turned, wind was never present.
This was testament to a way of addressing the world.

None of the clocks agreed.

Once she had been observed
sleeping beside a log on a beach.

The vehicle stands for the space between places.

She thought her ideas of concealment somehow equaled silence.

Her place of clocks and maps.

She particularly wanted to sleep.

If one waits or if one holds back or if one is exuberant
or if one insists.

Perhaps anything can or must be said.

The birds would remain
in the afternoon heat
if the breeze picked up
or the air were still.

An echo has three facets.

THE WAY THE ROOM SMELLS

The precision of any word or the way we use it, here, in the opposite of entry. I.e. pronouns torture us because they're proxies, they're points of contact; for example rumors, spying, breeches of trust. Or here, in the correlative of reason, we may agree on a concept, a production of histories. We find the recent blurry. Nor can grammar aid their procession, the prodigious flight, the diminutive call.

Though they came with intention others said volition.

They keep saying syntax but they mean money.

They pump gas but they could just go home.

Or the streets are washed with fervor.

In this way things are flush.

Their perfume carries in advance.

Her voice was familiar. Its timbre touched a chord.

The dialogues which we might compose
wrinkle too quickly.

Fatigue would sweep them away.
Their core temperatures would rob them.

They would willingly surrender.

Some say succumb.

As in a mood someone mentioned once in temper, in pressure
or a skyward superstition which hangs on.

Seasonally or, put another way,
measured by our own need to measure;
we are listening though reported unable.

For sure we have voted to keep the phone from the desk.

Thus sounds emanate or seem to emanate
from objects which ought to be solid.
To say that this causes worry would be overstatement.
But the tides are stronger than usual,
their neaps and springs energetic in a way
that alarms those who believe nature a person.

Perhaps we'd decide to remain away
if the planet were not so remote.

Our objects can't really deceive us.

The mocking bird's list carefully unwinding
like any detail carefully unwound.
It's neither space nor time unwinding.
No details lacking.

It's life can't be severed: these are only photos.

No sheet that loud, no twisted light source,
because if you want to read you will.
In some perfect state of denial or containment.
The sentence unwinds, the story, the animal.

Or those simple dreams
where the dog jumps over the bed
and you remember any act of love.

Here the voice by which we mean a northerly
prevailing by which we picture tundra gusted upon
who ain't a place or was that a different writer
mid-nineteenth century before the two-day warning
or the seven-second delay.

The prevailing voice but the vehicle, unclear and evasive,
is stethoscopic. It's time with or without lists
by whose function we thought perspective would be erased.
Just as the infinitive is anticipated – desired? –
or are we closer to a volcanic base by which we picture
basaltic landscapes too young for trees
heat still rising.

They weren't heeding the hour. The prevalent basaltic voice
pictured somehow as entwined by which self-sufficiency
springs to mind and concealment.

Here somehow figured. No picture is conjured.
By which place is meant to be released
which could mean voiced or would that be the opposite?
Here no one would expect a reason
which doesn't mean there is one,
through which door a backdrop is seen, windless,
like an anchor pull.

If any record is made, where *is* means
could or might be, the turn they heed
accepting one set of religions,
even their interruptions somehow sacrosanct.

Someone's *this veneer of appearance*
not nearly sufficient, this globe's *over and under*
not nearly sufficient to contain all its errors,
which means whose?

Nor is it the transparency of sound
but rather the expectation that what is ill
can be put right or that any memory
has roots in belief.

Please notice the placement of objects overly finished,
please notice that the way in which they speak
is meant to simulate record.

When the question arises and the hallways fill with light,
where light itself is not a concept,
what is seen in one place may not repeat elsewhere.

Though what is set down is not the same as setting right.
Please notice the conditional state of any penetrant.
The republic is enormous and rests on an alphabet.

The aroma they wished to impose would not linger.
The month had changed yet again.
The subject of heat was not appropriate
but remained on everyone's mind.

The demand was slack.
The dictionary's introduction unreal.
Sorrow is not so overwhelming. But in politics
we settle for the way the room smells.

A color was left as a marker. Some said crimson
others gray. Some called it a note
both missive and musical,
a signature, both mythic and paginated.
Content, she said, but in the sad way.
Or was that wise and sad, a child distracted?

Now any information must be doubted.
The motives are too strong
but the implications seem obvious,
a deck between island and mainland,
gulls in tow but also flying, pictured instead.

They had guessed at his whereabouts. Their concern
was in their own body of knowledge.

The lore is startling.

COMPOUNDED CAPITALS

His quill so temporary. But the sound of it on paper.
Buried in eddies of cloud the sunlight, the capitals of columns.
Fate's runaway slave. Sleeves too big.

The air is heavy that settles in cuts.

Physically only a visitor, and yet not unpleased.
Furniture set in the center of the room so the periphery
could be paced, without light, at any time or weather.

Shoulders may be put level.
The buried water is warm but dense.

Some claimed any keepsake to be a thing they called an archetype. Yet others divine footsteps from adjoining properties, such as the universal solvency of water, or career hopes dashed to terrazzo floors. Still others hear someone in a gambling hall, making a killing, pockets full of gemstones, hands full of rough cut.

The phase they call exchange is mistaken for justice, prejudice or the acumen of brokers. Tables of reference are razed or embellished. Try the lights and test the plumbing, take dimensions and see a future.

Finality is seen slowly sometimes.

Where, if they had come to the crossing of desire and the behavior which causes desire's defeat, a comet had been rumored but not seen. These had been projections, what men in lab coats hire illustrators to portray. The country was younger; the expectations unsullied. She sang Wenceslaus incessantly, the occasion not really of importance. But the rhythms were scary, the argument being something about translation.

Their interjections were always more interesting than their footnotes.

And yet exuberance, in any form, can also catalyze withdrawal.

Somewhere the procession stops, or was that process?

Dreams migrate from the interior, where Clytemnestra prowls in disbelief. Sacrifice and vigilance mar the background they form. A tiny goddess steals to the furthest frontier.

Thus boxed, or rather the ocean, increasing in swell, the very openness they must have read of once, an incarnate idea, or rather any thing as disembodied as space, or re-embodied, localized to the point of arousal, or so we comfort ourselves.

Even the rising fantasy, even the faint legacy of a family vanishing.

We cannot see the lightning but we cannot stop thinking of revenge or at least we think of parity but we cannot see the reason which is how they might explain the language they develop that strives to obscure actions. And it may be a simple shift in barometric pressure, where blood and ink and water spring easily and smoothly, because they know of our attachments to sensation. We have begun to believe that, because their abilities have erased the marks and crosshatchings, anything residual is regressive. Forward, thus, loses its relativity. Or so says their vigilant language.

It was the light before the rain or during the gathering or it was a music from an earlier time tainted in ways we can't know now, or so we compound our interests.

THE FRAMED CITY

Though he had reported once before
on the viscous nature of still water,
there were those who read it differently.
Others had chosen to permanently mark their flesh.
There had been no further steps to decline the novel.

Some found the redundancies intolerable:
not the repeating of subjects but the paths to get there;
not the irreversibility of any action
but the affirmation that the brain is physical so it's all physical.

The boys played their gun play still,
yet the obesity of their children never seemed connected.

This was the house of repetition where everything was incipient.

They dip beneath a sheet of light, weightless and breathless
doubting the preponderances and spaces
that they themselves contain.

You are steep and steep also means tight.
Then sleep can be sexual.
Thus textures become olfactory.
Efficiency is a crucial factor,
the precepts, marked and annotated,
career, like the sorrow of billiards.

The sentences we inhale
leave only a trace.

But they have given us melodies
to displace thoughts.
We dream of a ship
on its side, careening.

No matter how desperate the words, the translation appears
desperately below, in matters uncalm.

Perhaps because the nature of any single thing
seems inconstant, memories, for example,
memories or the chain of events which lead to intervention.

To intervene could also be to counsel caution:
fish usually cannot fly, the plural isn't often singular.
Or physically, as one conversation
may be said to intervene,
from the air, for example,
we come upon a train of thought,
a chain of events,
an incarnadine pattern of speech.

Elusive is the quality of any single thing.

In the barometric world examples would be less important.
The schools travel predictably.
A gift is not a gift but a code to be deciphered.
Cement steps replace sand at the shoreline and city
encroaches in narrow streets up to the steps.

A minaret would not surprise us. Its voice, not uncalm,
actually singular.

They dream their home near water, where everything counts.
If otherwise noted in other books
the dreamland's hidden, a fortress expository.
Their sweet model posits a climate of change,
a report we now recall.

Their state of grace is less pacific.
Or each state has its own logic.

Theirs is finished in blue tones;
deaf as if alone in a vacant fantasy,
because the music they set in,
each beat, each pad
tipped, dreamed in the lumbar spine.

The picture is framed: the European City.

The other frame is vast beyond pattern.

The first stage was raked because the city's American and America is steep.

The voice of police pervades any interior.

Assistance is a ticklish thing. Attraction also.

Now tell us of the legend. The legend is sometimes keyed to a color, sometimes to texture.

It's hard to see the transactional as subtle, unless it is scripted.

Lines may also be used. The legend is keyed to smell. Metal also has an odor.

In Europe they all know each other but walking is unimpeded. This is one city.

Hills are accounted for. The legend is corporal. An arch may be useful. We'll opt for paper.

A wall is a wall. The stage is flat. The grid will remain invisible this time.

Frame and recognition are more texture than taste.

Gold will be used as emphasis.

Even attraction can be complicated.

STUDIES IN FOURTEEN LINES
2010

I

If It's Only Rhythm

Because a thermal motif heard
in the hands of a Bedouin child
you cannot allow to guide you.

Sure, we've waited a decade
or a millennium to find a system of letters.

This is a story where only air is solved.

The metals that cover other metals
or ceramics that cushion high voltage
or how can you just lie there and listen
when the whole coast is lit?

Your face that burned so many eyelids.

If it's only rhythm then what's the dew point?
As if following a procedure ignites
a point of fire on every peak.

Miles of Ocean (with Markers)

Rescue, ideal or actual
is only a story, a line.

Not that the name of something must be its fate
or that the real meaning of a line can't be its sound.

Attempting to cross the lines
routes were found, circuitous but uncertain.

Every time you've traveled the plane has crashed.
Every train has derailed, each car exploded.
Each disaster cradles the next
a painted Russian toy you return to.

Then only the image of a fading wake will stand as marker
if there is such an image and even if there were
only your shadow would be seen.

It's what we think we saw that sends us with rope or buoy.

Water Tablet (with Fire)

The volcano's spigot submerged
then the calm blue imprint,
then the dolphin's high-pitched marrow.

You create your own quest
or boil all day in the shadow of blued fire.

It pleases us to so reconstruct
as if there could be a reconstruction.
As if the game were open.

From a tiny booklet
the fear bleeds out

but only the passengers know it.
As if the passengers were incapable of steering.

If there could only be an imprint
because at first they jump into the water.

Alternate Use

Not that something's name must be its fate
or the sound it makes in the years they make
for example taking the wrong person's car
or freezing the milk but these are small
things compared to looking at photos from
anyone's past and feeling remorse or nostalgia
in the same way that a razor left on the counter
might be used in another context to
trim a carcass or shave a face not
the exception like futile glass cutting
or the romance of not receiving or giving up.
It could be the responsibility of the sentimental
or the doubt inspired by the real meaning
of a line stalled between sound and accumulation.

Street (with Voices)

Who they were, or that she spoke.
Open windows but it's raining.
Police reports but the air is round.

In other words
the street is bombed out or demolished.
Whoever had done it there was still a way
immune to damage
or she spoke going west, turning south.

The gate is whole, the dangers vague.
The conversation turns east;
A square orbit will be just anomalous enough.

No matter the turns or the sealed reports
or what you make of either
voices enter

A Thin Covering (with Ceiling)

When suddenly it dawned on me
because the sun had never entered into it before
and now a very white old woman
dripped blood onto this young man's hand.

It's like everything going completely silent
and then you open a drawer and all the usual sounds
rush out startling and bass.
I should have said new.

She kept saying
"What is it that you're trying to do?"
and my hands were almost under control.

After all who can see everything that happens?
Or what rises has more to do with fluids and tissues,
where the issue of sight folds dark and under.

An Island City

Not that notes were taken
across the fierce and woody table.
They don't reply when asked for opinions
this far from the wind-smoothed plane.
They are distracted by weightiness.

Because the air at this hour in a radiant move
withholds an expected message
pushing the possibility of torture; too enticing.
The courtly mouth dripping blood onto the white-gloved hand
you can't expect this to go on without comment.

Here then. Across the hollow table.
An hour has drawn up to the cold gate.
Bids are made; to open, to keep closed.
The recorder is shut off. The discs keep spinning.

Returning (with Boon)

It ends up here again
no claims or excuses
typed against a grain pandered to
confirmed, rewarded, just like before.

It falls away; the scene
where they take you to a ritual confession
where the pallid priests read Chinese
without excuse or claim.

Don't talk to me about the complexities:
I saw the water bleeding from the seams
of your linen jacket. I watched the puddles dry
and the footsteps and the extra syllables.

Don't allude to this. Let it rest.
The bristle of sea water, the burrowing fish.

Anxiety of Stereoscopy

One day your vision bends around an obstacle.
Now the fish can see you up from under,
or you see her eyes relax from across a table.

To be full of color means excitement.
Cones and rods
now form a new kind of detail.

Her cliff dwelling armor but that's only a joke.
There's a huge pool of fog settled into the city
but nothing any of us can't shunt or block.

Yet the white city shimmers
as if someone dreamed this
as if the filter would simply dissolve.

It's not some dull phrase or take notes on this
until the meaning or the invitation comes clear.

Assembly

You might think the announcer had influence.
There are twelve images sounding with hope
transferred twelve times
noted, copied, voiced.

Even the gardens are loaded with ideology.
The announcer is discreet.

This might have been an aquarium once.
The vast stretch of blacktop is now said merely to wait.

Color is the casualty.

The voice, rimed objective,
alludes to patterns and histories.

It describes a vast taxonomy of food.
It reminds us that, earlier,
the dogma had been soundly submerged.

Despite Intervention

To only judge them by their fashions
would titillate a commentator too distant
too difficult to imagine.

The soft lighting of their grand room
the foliage by day the image of them sophisticated
by night.

I have heard the motto on their coat of arms
read rhythmically in tony groupings
but no one smiled.

No matter how carefully the books are anchored
certain of them are kept by distinguished guests
as souvenirs.

There is a hole in the top of the story. The fabric
is folded neatly in the field, safe from nearly everyone.

Antecedent (with Problem)

As if a storm opened a clarity
the metaphor is air plus psyche.

The question is about form:
how far to carry which bucket.

And yet the mosquito
that wakes you takes with it
the world you were in.

To personify would help the fable
but infer something about mosquitoes
that you can't know.

Nor the pronoun "you" in this case
meaning to be möbiuslike
opening when closing, inside when out.
And then the problem of psyche as soul.

2

Civics (with First Person)

It would be a dry and primal day at the capitol.
I have altered the course of my gaze
to enclose an entire room but avoid
a single passageway.

No matter how many times I look up
I hear continuity, a comforting rhythm
like a story but of course there is none.

Maybe there's a centrifuge to keep adherence minimal
or a government with all its weight and people.

I become the witness.
I wait to see who assumes the table's head
and who volunteers to hold the four posts outside.

In a cadence we can't deny, in a system I've encouraged,
listen, I'd tell them. Wait, I'd tell them.

Nostos (with Signal)

Twenty years later when he visited again
if that was location then this is response:

The bundle of certain and uncertain conduits,
the balance of certain chemicals, but hold that thought:
several groomed and able people have entered.
"It must be winter my coat has grown long,"
says the first one, though giving off
a certain redolence of allegory
no matter what the scale is called.

In an ore too fine, on a cold central peak
we are waiting for a signal
and the meek are lifting their fingers
because to beckon might disturb someone
and those bonfires along the shore are not the sign.

Cutting Beckett

There will be no one at the cathedral.
My son is peeping from behind the bushes.
And I had hoped for fair weather
but definitely it's raining.

The boat on a day like this
so much like an island
so much like an echo.

What news do they bring from the north?

An incessant worry
that the map will be the ruler.
Can you picture that?
Because a line of people now call for you.

The quality of the gesture will not make sense.
Would that be time? Then volume perhaps.

Kinch

Cut the pear or I cut the pear.
She wouldn't say it was spoiled but, like syntax,
the beginning was different from the end.

As at other times a scene
rendered from a dream
or a distant memory recurs:
The low, bleached coastal town,
the labyrinthine train tunnels,
a kind of herd but voices.

Is it syntax that's stored as a sugar,
or with diffidence as protein's residue?
Which synapse emboldens
under the shade of passing jet wings
then dives backward, away from the map they impose?

Elusive Architecture (with Figures)

While the sodden old bogs cavorted in the front room
elsewhere water heated.
Or erase that and add an evening according to custom.
Make it courtly, mannered, ancient.
Yet, despite your every effort
a military inference can't be expunged.

But in a foreground rendered tangible
the old ones yield the floor
while elsewhere something boils.

The invisible ground's voice-over
tries to explain background as abstraction
but the guests are engaged against the proof of boiling.

Somewhere in the middle an approach becomes possible.
A solid concession. Hold high the burial feathers.

Full Moon (with Shadow)

I have collected all the papers
and stacked them and held the ball of twine
listening to crows and waiting for the moon's eclipse.

There must be a scenario.

What agency compels us toward consensus,
that understands halfway
as destiny?

What agency assumes that swelling Albinoni
and dissolving pastorality will
convince us of anything?

I have wound and unwound the twine.

Instead of gestures
the moon diminishes by a
moment's gibbous bite.

Sant' Egidio

Wanting only dogma
asleep at the master's elbow
the city always white

vineyards pictured when someone mentions surface
wanting only postcards of towers
of open cities where only arrivals are remarked

roadearly fog banks
Umbrian fields by the city's shimmer
wanting a certain doctrinal air
steps mid-mountain to the gates

"The doors are locked," a helper says.
"Tonight the owners eat with us.
"Their grand table's inside the toolshed.
"Knock tomorrow. Someone will answer."

Night Sirens

As you may have written
when the question came up
across a neutral backdrop

as you may have asked,
neutrally, listening, or
when gossip, treachery, release
conjured danger or sound

as you might have asked yourself
as the revelers acted without you
your phrases, your terms, your forms
centered but invisible

or against neutral background,
had the weather's pressure yielded
clean examples, clear tests.

Property (with Fragments)

But on the tour (notice the wood work).

Brinkley's view not always heliocentric.

Manning the lifeboats in this case accurate.

A drink preferred but put off by millions.

How, in the cycle of Vico, could they?

Somewhere in the middle an approach becomes possible.

Frequency was only one unempirical way of posting concern.

They saw the innovative pillars carved in their hometown trees.

Would the idea of siderealcentrism make more sense?

What news do they bring from the north?

Imagine how significant the architecture could be.

And there's that feeling again, as if read, as if dreamed.

Vineyards pictured when someone mentions surface.

As if anything were certain, no matter how often.

Recombinant Only On Paper

Hear me he said to listen I fear the seamless.
The merchants were coming and no time to lose.

You have traveled their stairways
and even your friends seemed ready to sell.

This needn't be the blockade feared by historical projectionists.

In the land of parallels you broke the wall.

It's so dark outside, the fence so far away.

A shining dog eats a penny
and rain clouds gather on a distant edge.

They have lit a fire and the air smells of creosote.

This might have been an aquarium once.
The vast stretch of blacktop should seem smaller now.

Copy only a sound or hope they remember.
Imagine how significant a frenzied pack of dogs.

3

Cover

Here's your tempting overture
a color transformed to taste
but we mean social judgment
or a cobalt vapor trail
because really what we mean is boundary.

A familiar voice
yet suspect.

All these moments of keen
interest to the listeners.
But they have been displaced.
The image of a helicopter gunship
bleeds out, but stays.

Here's your color
transferred not traced.

Tunnels Seen

But now it's too late.
The deadline passed, even the clarity is gone.

The dream of a stranger giving birth
is just an idea you borrowed.

They report on wildfires
but the chain is unbroken, an etymology.

These are not excavations.
Everything is extemporized.

The flag burning on the cover of your essay
burns quickly.

What can we tell them when the sheets are so wet?
That the drive now exceeds the gravity?
That the forest, like a missed grasp,
is denatured?

If Another Word

You can wash down a memory,
tow certain masters (or their shades)
to be your focus or tokens, be measured
and forgotten in the honest zones,
but only by a special map,
one that succumbs
to tides and eclipses,
air supplies and territory
but never to logistics, never to ambition.

Did they combine your sounds or threaten to?
Did the example of their viscous light impede
the memory of the stairs or cancel the image
of slipping into a fluid you want to remember
but know you can't?

Five Things Imagined (with Maps)

Imagine a language carried by volition.
Imagine idea as desire.

For example, imagine the course
she might have followed and her foot's
impression in soil or mud or sand.

Imagine being jealous of the food someone likes.

They will touch a tender arm
and the lights will not go on.

Maps will turn yellow and red: routes followed,
rhythms, syntax, denotations observed.

"But the chart's a landscape.
They've ignited a fire and the air is marked."

Won't somebody help them?

Imagine being jealous of the terraced road to get there.

Turning (with Sound)

Music on an island's saturated air.
Nothing can dry.
Triads don't form an armature.

It's either a bell or a bowl that rings.

Launched from the platform
invoked in chants,
impaneled witnesses perform the true journey.
There is no logic now nor taste.

An aroma revives time,
the bowl or bell's minor chime
a promise that decays into air
or an imperfection on endless ocean:
an inert canopy, unrestrained,
a veil we dare not lift.

Gawain

Her slip into monaural
though falls were regional
and cuts landmarks.

Finger lakes
trusting the effect of directions
or dark green sectors
summer, history, place.

On her insistence
or on her bed

and just when erasure
and memory lapse.

Palm to the black floor.
Who's listening?
And the books hidden in her purse.

Sudden Crisis (with Lacunae)

A "blustery winter's day" is conjured.
Who would have the audacity to ask about subject?

They had whistled and I had rehearsed.

Mail came and everything in the house was sorted.
Thus, you might have remembered me
in the middle of your involving dream.

His last sensation rising.

Seascape (with Travelers)

First hearing on the outlands' side,
as if the stream unleashed the romantic image,
cracking cheeks, the analytic caption.
Thus the color, the rock spines, the tidal fury.

They stand at the sea shore, then,
because they couldn't stop talking
or may have changed their minds.

They are listed but not aboard,
as if what they said had meaning
action becomes a hope they remember.

What if their windows had the southern light?
What if they knew the hand that listed them?
Could there be an image in sound?

Ahead, around, the ocean basin, steel surface.

Gravel's Edge

Trout mouths:
water color.

You thought breech
but breech was the exception.

Swirling surface;
laked silence.

To be lifted into suffocation
by unarticulated child hands

Dorsal ridges arch
breech oily surface

wind erases, stipples

tongueless mouths
water color

silent spines.

Presage

We had expected a messenger,
a broken point piercing a difficult passage.

You have left a tincture.

Beside the lamp sound was heard.
The notations or fragments were found on an island.

We opened the door with a word not a pickax.

It wasn't paper we expected.
Yet gangs will appear.

We don't *see* any of this.
Prepositions never agree from place to place.
But now it's too late.
We understand each sentence.

Then what did we bring?
Who was the messenger this time?

STUDY FOR THE POSSIBILITY OF HOPE
2010

It's light on a wall or a conference table
not the window in the palace framing the hoi polloi.
It's the music and the absence of shadows that gives it away.

The goal would be to touch an object one dimensional,
cells, for example, or a mountain range.

You say this is an illusion. Then the bulb shatters
and the window's only a painting, a world of relief.

An amoeba splits. Colors shift from one to the next.
Now there are four.

There's not quite a rhythm, not quite a dance.

You try to pin the moment
and the moment disappears.

There's also a flower called Proteus:
a story or a trick of the eye?

Benevolence looks for an outcome.
Benevolence precipitates as a vestige of hope.

Any shred can root here, given the right combination.
Any shred is epic, or could be.

That is to say, bring the crying baby into bed or let her cry in
    terror,
there's always the hope of undoing previous outcomes.

Sweet water tricks the eyes of donors.

Somehow the ceiling of cloud fills me with hope.
You say the deck is peeling and the sails are frayed.
You live in a different world.

Someone tells us that the mountains are not a wall but an axis.
Another says they're too thick to be either.

The streets are wide here where the patrol cars are seldom.
The gun in the closet a muted center of gravity.

Alternate routes deflect a planet. Air adheres to it.
Mass becomes our private joke
as in the displacement of money effected by work.

This is when the heat wave breaks into cold snap and the layers
gray and chill, barricade the outward view,
funnel a wind northerly enough to alarm custom
as if we thought the global exempt from its parts.

That fog hangs from the valley's rim
by spindles with eyehooks;

That the rim is uncommonly even
and the wind that visits is always from the west;

That the voice describing the scene renders it artifice
and the vista a shell and brittle;

Assume that the route, thick as plaster, will vanish.

If by route a method is implied, of transport for example,
then the rows of cast steel wouldn't be enough
to make a raft with, or rake the waters calm;
one shipwreck's direct line is another's stormy sea.

I kiss the back of Arete's knees, her husband the wiser.
"This is only conveyance," we all think,
the valley's shell bending down, a blanket, as it were.

Two birds appear on two rims.
There is a dust of snow on the mountains behind them.
By them I mean the olive trees growing inside the rims.
It's mid April in this desert basin people keep insisting upon.
They are finches, and appear as if condensed from the clouds.
There was a time when their presence would require augury.
By time I mean the chain of mountain valleys, each one drier
    than the next.

The basin is drier than its dwellers want to know.
When snow melts it needs to go somewhere.
The readers of snow's residue are rare in these parts.

In summer a spot of mud can bake solid and ceramic.

They who brought water are remembered by dry roads and journals.
Privately we mark their passage with cups of enameled sheet-metal
that amplify icy runoff even in heat.

Why suddenly a calm presides
try it later they signal the way across arroyos running
the desert's exception, three blind trail heads,
foliage gathered around the trace of water's passage.
By running something consecutive was implied,
liquid being rarer than continuity or locomotion.
Later they stopped they said, vastness here, vestiges.

The tributaries' calm is thermal.
Sounds drop off muffled by heat.
The branches can't be sourced.

Pass through with your water guarded and flasked.

The single thing you need to fear is air.
A ribbon of pavement, fractured
and eroded, is only a witness.

Sound is frightening.
So are distance and magnitude.
So is the pinpoint. So is the whisper.

The agora is a dangerous place.
People claim territory in the smallest ways and the fiercest.

I said, "Look at the mountains. You can't touch them."
"Mountains," you said, new to the language of words.

When the pillow is the point of a pin and a massive granite slab,
run through the neighborhood looking for safety.
Avoid the station wagon from which newspapers fly.
It may be necessary to strike a bargain:
voices whisper their hollering.
What does it mean to reset the cycle?
In lieu of evasion learn their names.

This highway's Sunday just endless enough
to support any quiet idea of sovereignty.

By highway I mean a long paved road that hurries commerce.

Then there are the patches of black ice or the sudden walls of fog
    supporting what? Immanence?
Or do danger and fatality justify the production of history to order?

By order I mean thirteen people sitting at table
rehearsing their assumption of escape and redemption.

Your house in a ring of gum trees
alone on a desert ridge a mile of dirt and gravel
enough to keep things separate.

Where are the poems I wrote that set your scene?
Even more, who are you, and why have you allowed me
to use your isolation as examples of my own?

Where did those pages go? Who rehearses the steps of their loss?

I say to you why are you shouting and you shout louder
but these are not your tidings and the rules are just barely mine.

Your face is also in the convex rear-view, sleeping or making
    peace with nouns.

That mountains loom before our careening car
is a care you can't bow to, the side views
teeming with names.

Rest heavy in the sling you make of my arms; I'll watch the
    range for now.

I can accept that you'll see in me the face of the bourgeoisie
and that claims for lean and acetic postures might ring hollow,
   somewhat.

Yours will be an arena I can't fathom from here
not even knowing what here will be then.

There was a song from before you or I were born
that said "When today is a long time ago."

I think of that often when I think of you.

You see the jumble of nouns fit into something,
find actions, find resonance, then the world contracts and explodes
and I mean this in a good way because notions of hope
are about continuing, just as any anticipation anticipates death.
That is to say future anticipates a sentence if not a phrase.

It is better to leave these things alone but that's just a portal,
the construction of which anticipates the past.

She said, I just think of myself as a boat
moored in a glassy cove.

She might have said raft
and been thinking of currents and mercy

or, looking up from a coral bottom,
of "the vessel, the shadow of the vessel, the shadow alone."

Languid river up there, slow surface.

Author's Note

The Hero Is Nothing (1985), Kajun Books, San Francisco. *Hero* was the first and last book that Kajun published. Patricia Koren and Jeanne Jambu publishers.

A World (1989), Sun and Moon Press, Los Angeles. The first of four books of poetry and a novel published by Douglas Messerli's press.

Arena (1991), Sun and Moon Press. *Arena* completes a loose trilogy with *The Hero Is Nothing* and *A World*.

20 Questions (1992), Jahbone Press, Los Angeles. Martin Nakell published this book as the second in his series, which began with Leland Hickman's *Lee Sr. Falls to the Floor*.

Book of Hours (1996), ML&NLF, Piacenza, Italy. This is a collaborative work with artist Courtney Gregg, published by Michele Lombardelli, and translated into Italian by Franco Nasi.

Credence (1996), Sun and Moon Press. *Credence* builds on the use of prose in *20 Questions* (combined with an ongoing study of the lyric) in the first of three sections, the second and third of which are footnotes to the previous two.

Study for the Ideal City (1999), Seeing Eye Books, Los Angeles, published in Guy Bennett's long-standing chapbook series. This study is one of three written in the span of time covered by this volume. The first is represented here as *Studies in Fourteen Lines*, but its original composition predates *Study for the Ideal City*.

Sand (2002), Green Integer, Los Angeles. This press is Douglas Messerli's reincarnation of Sun and Moon Press.

Studies in Fourteen Lines (2010), Echo Park Press, Los Angeles, limited edition published by Lizzy Epstein, with drawings by John Millei. Like the other two studies, it was composed using a modest formal restraint. Unlike the other two, though, it has gone through a series of revisions, recombinations, additions and deletions over a span of 19 years, taking advantage of its circuitous path to publication. It is published here in its entirety.

Study for the Possibility for Hope (2010), Pie in the Sky Press, Simi Valley, CA. This is a limited edition, letterpress book designed, printed and bound by Rebecca Chamlee. It is the last written of the three studies, and consists of etudes composed before the daily work on the novel, *Hope*. It too is published here in its entirety.

Appearance-fields: Dennis Phillips's Navigation

George Albon

In *The Hero Is Nothing,* Dennis Phillips's first book of poetry, its writer becomes restless and pictures "the wingbeats and accompaniment/ of Sunday Morning." He is thinking of Stevens's early poem, its coffee and oranges, its "complacencies of the peignoir." The older poet's couple happily steep themselves in the secular sun of a comfortable room, in which the poet-husband abjures the rote devotions that would run fullness like this through a mesh of dead codes. If Stevens has a metaphysics, it is a metaphysics of solidity. He was able to write his own charter because of an opulent church of self that was its own greatest dominion. The church of self also allowed him to find a place for his iotas, a commodious worldly sanctum for the patient unfolding of detail and assertion. Over fifty years later an American poet searches to find a place for his iotas without a church of self, without a table on which to put the planet, but on the run, in fugitive spaces where matter doesn't rest but shifts implications. Not parts of a world but a world of parts. Not lost, not bereft, but in a discomfort of suspension, and the other side of complacency. One must navigate as best one can.

The later poet's coordinates – elegance, balance, surprise – might indeed evoke a strange relation with the author of "Sunday Morning." Along with the accompaniment, however, are the wingbeats, crisp but fleeting, gathering sound as they disperse location. But a line in a poem, like a question answered: "If that was location then this is response." The task becomes attention to the message of import as displayed in disparate space, like a juggler's pins caught in freeze-frame. Phillips's work is a foot-forward gesture in the midst of a specific modernity's atomistic waywardness; the labors involved are intuitive and painstaking, as befits searching in fractured light. His is the great contemporary poetry of epistemology in crisis.

Before they were parts of tales, gods wrote mortals. Books like *A World* are situated amid convenience stores and atavistic wars, and look back—not at the golden ages, but some time-in-breech after the gold fell off, when mortals tried to fight like gods and couldn't, and squinted harder to see their superiors. Battle is sorting it out, except it isn't. It's war as anatomized by Simone Weil, and warriors as leaping salmon. The Empyrean is being appealed to by adrenalin, its celestial features growing fainter with every terrestrial hormone spike. Finally, "nothing is solved./ Only the arena enlarges." The arena that enlarges is conflict, but there might be a flicker of other possibility, something "sunny and populous," if we read it as "except that the arena enlarges." That is, that the interpretive center has put down roots and by growing larger is opening new ground. Ground to study rather than conquer. The next book is called *Arena*.

Pound begins a book with "And." A section in a book by Phillips begins with "But." The modernist inclination to see all cultures and eras as coeval has become a (   )-modern accounting of features and behaviors. That second world is just as big as the first, but it is a world in relay—of information, of compressed communication. ("The foreground is shadowed by glimpses/ populated by things that have been taken.") One can imagine lines of such poetry as strips of paper, missives rather than fortunes, passed on to the next contact. And yet this is a relay that creates circumference, exposing so many facets of the problematic that a new path has appeared. "Awake in my own fire/ I create the world."

The superscript numbers and letters of *Credence* are not pedantic; nor, as material, are they ironic. They mark the drop-point of phenomenological plumb lines; they offer site, rather than cite. ("There is a hole in the top of the story," we read, in another book.) Think of the symbological weave in Sufi texts, where symbols aren't one-to-one pairings, but vibrational nodes that will occur to different readers on different points of the continuum. This work's footnotes and their offspring are experiential rather than directive; there should be an increasing hum as they are neared.

Throughout the work, throughout the books, the consciousness of the moment of time, but that moment rarely revealing its notch in a timeline. Stevens's jar made the wilderness surround it; it bent the world to its singularity. But what seems place-taking in Stevens is haunted by temporality in Phillips. There is rarely a moment when something remarked on in a poem is not contingent to something else, exerting a pull on the first thing and making it part of a warping sequence, just as the some-thing else must also yield gravity to the appearance-field of the new arrival. One could in fact experience the work – line, poem, book, selection – as a progress of appearance-fields. Phillips has been able to oversee a dynamic process for this action/reaction with his customization of the serial poem, where the sequential-revelatory character of individual poems unfolds its own natural macrostructure.

As first appearance, so first witness. Travel – its intensities of encounter, its flashes of life as sign – is a crucial act throughout. Travel is the supreme "thrower-together" of space and time, of the local and the rapid, of the quick veering of appearance into consequence. Coast, beach, mountain, island. Frequently-used words. "Everything was incipient," from a book called *Sand*. Places gotten to, places left, places lodged in the mind. And other words, city, history, weather. All experience as heightened, as it is in new found land. "They dream their house near water, where everything counts." And yet aren't all coastal people visitors?

The last two collections in this volume are "studies." One title sounds self-reflexive, *Studies in Fourteen Lines*, and the other, *Study for the Possibility of Hope*, anything but. But this is chime-rical. The former searches every bit as conscientiously for paths among facts as the latter, which in its turn could have been called "Studies in Seven Lines." When the investigation is conducted as here, the visionary and the scholastic are one. There's the story of 19th century naturalist Louis Agassiz making his students study the specimen – a fish, I believe – again and again, over and over, over and again. He was teaching them to note but he was really teaching them to bind. With accretion you see around to the back of things. And in a work like *Twenty Questions*, which is all recom-binant accretion (twenty "questions" per section, none of them interrogative), the statements and their implications mount and escalate and merge in such a way that what becomes important is the momentum of noticing and noting, rather than a resolution to go along with the sentence structure. Among the profuse markers of an increasingly termless world you must testify in an uncommon key. Things live different; you begin to understand enrichment.

Can this telegraphic log entry, at the end of a remarkable volume, let slip an unfashionable word? Can I mention that *Navigation*, and the poetry of Dennis Phillips in general, along with its finely-modulated unquiet, its grace under pressure, its intellective/affective generosity over three decades of rock-steady writing, and the cache of qualities still to be discovered there – can I say, also, that it is lovely? The way red sky at morning is lovely, if not the first thing a mariner wants to see? I'll let the captain of this particular vessel take over.

> ...if Wittgenstein says that philosophy
> must be as complex as the knots it seeks to unravel
> then poetry must be a knot, beautiful and impossible
> that instead of needing to be untangled,
> of its own accord blooms.

Other titles from Otis Books | Seismicity Editions

Erik Anderson, *The Poetics of Trespass*
    Published 2010 | 112 Pages | $12.95
    ISBN-13: 978-0-979-6177-7-5
    ISBN-10: 0-979-6166-7-4

J. Reuben Appelman, *Make Loneliness*
    Published 2008 | 84 pages | $12.95
    ISBN-13: 978-0-9796177-0-6
    ISBN-10: 0-9796177-0-7

Bruce Bégout, *Common Place. The American Motel.*
    Published 2010 | 143 Pages | $12.95
    ISBN-13: 978-0-979-6177-8-2
    ISBN-10: 0-979-6177-8-

Guy Bennett, *Self-Evident Poems*
    Published 2011 | 96 pages | $12.95
    ISBN-13: 978-0-9845289-0-5
    ISBN-10: 0-9845289-0-3

Guy Bennett and Béatrice Mousli, Editors, *Seeing Los Angeles:
A Different Look at a Different City*
    Published 2007 | 202 pages | $12.95
    ISBN-13: 978-0-9755924-9-6
    ISBN-10: 0-9755924-9-1

Robert Crosson, *Signs/ & Signals: The Daybooks of Robert Crosson*
    Published 2008 | 245 Pages | $14.95
    ISBN: 978-0-9796177-3-7

Robert Crosson, *Daybook (1983–86)*
    Published 2011 | 96 Pages | $12.95
    ISBN-13: 978-0-9845289-1-2
    ISBN- 0-9845289-1-1

Ray DiPalma, *The Ancient Use of Stone:
Journals and Daybooks, 1998–2008*
    Published 2009 | 216 pages | $14.95
    ISBN: 978-0-9796177-5-1

Jean-Michel Espitallier, *Espitallier's Theorem*
Translated from the French by Guy Bennett
Published 2003 | 137 pages | $12.95
ISBN: 0-9755924-2-4

Leland Hickman, *Tiresias: The Collected Poems of Leland Hickman*
Published 2009 | 205 Pages | $14.95
ISBN: 978-0-9822645-1-5

Norman M. Klein, *Freud in Coney Island and Other Tales*
Published 2006 | 104 pages | $12.95
ISBN: 0-9755924-6-7

Ken McCullough, *Left Hand*
Published 2004 | 191 pages | $12.95
ISBN: 0-9755924-1-6

Béatrice Mousli, Editor, *Review of Two Worlds:
French and American Poetry in Translation*
Published 2005 | 148 pages | $12.95
ISBN: 0-9755924-3-2

Ryan Murphy, *Down with the Ship*
Published 2006 | 66 pages | $12.95
ISBN: 0-9755924-5-9

Eric Priestley, *For Keeps*
Published 2009 | 264 pages | $12.95
ISBN: 978-0-979-6177-4-4

Ari Samsky, *The Capricious Critic*
Published 2010 | 240 pages | $12.95
ISBN-13: 978-0-979-177-6-8
ISBN: 0-979-6177-6-6

Hélène Sanguinetti, *Hence This Cradle*
Translated from the French by Ann Cefola
Published 2007 | 160 pages | $12.95
ISBN: 970-0-9755924-7-2

Janet Sarbanes, *Army of One*
> Published 2008 | 173 pages | $12.95
> ISBN-13: 978-0-9796177-1-3
> ISBN-10: 0-9796177-1-5

Severo Sarduy, *Beach Birds*
Translated from the Spanish by Suzanne Jill Levine
and Carol Maier
> Published 2007 | 182 pages | $12.95
> ISBN: 978-9755924-8-9

Adriano Spatola, *The Porthole*
Translated from the Italian by Beppe Cavatorta and Polly Geller
> Published 2011 | 112 pages | $12.95
> ISBN 13: 978-0-9796177-9-9
> ISBN-10: 0-9796177-9-0

Adriano Spatola, *Toward Total Poetry*
Translated from the Italian by Brendan W. Hennessey
and Guy Bennett
with an Introduction by Guy Bennett
> Published 2008 | 176 pages | $12.95
> ISBN 13: 978-0-9796177-2-0
> ISBN-10: 0-9796177-3-1

Carol Treadwell, *Spots and Trouble Spots*
> Published 2004 | 176 pages | $12.95
> ISBN: 0-9755924-0-8

Allyssa Wolf, *Vaudeville*
> Published 2006 | 82 pages | $12.95
> ISBN: 0-9755924-4-0